Anna Shepeard

D1415276

CIVIL WAR
in the Indian Territory

CIVIL WAR
in the
Indian Territory

Steve Cottrell
Illustrated by Andy Thomas

PELICAN PUBLISHING COMPANY
Gretna 1998

Copyright © 1995
By Steve Cottrell
All rights reserved

Art and illustrations © 1995
By Andy Thomas

First printing, 1995
Second printing, 1998

The word "Pelican" and the depiction of a pelican are trademarks
of Pelican Publishing Company, Inc.,
and are registered in the U.S. Patent and Trademark Office.

Library of Congress Cataloging-in-Publication Data

Cottrell, Steve.
    Civil War in the Indian Territory / Steve Cottrell ; foreword by
Whit Edwards ; illustrated by Andy Thomas.
        p.   cm.
    Includes bibliographical references and index.
    ISBN 1-56554-110-3 (pbk.)
    1. Indians of North America—Indian Territory—History.   2. Five
Civilized Tribes—History.   3. Indian Territory—History—Civil War,
1861-1865.   I. Title.
E78.I5C67   1995
976.65—dc20
                                                        95-2484
                                                        CIP

Illustration on pages 2-3: *The soldiers made their desperate stand against*
the overwhelming number of Osage warriors.

Manufactured in the United States of America

Published by Pelican Publishing Company, Inc.
P.O. Box 3110, Gretna, Louisiana 70054-3110

In February 1862, a 40-year-old farmer named Daniel Jennings enlisted in the 6th Kansas Cavalry Regiment at Fort Scott, Kansas. His brief but violent service in the U.S. Army brought him into contact with Native Americans in Indian Territory as well as in Arkansas and Missouri. Sometimes the Indians were his allies, other times his foes, and frequently they were both; different tribes, different units, different sides. Daniel's term of enlistment came to a sudden end when he was killed in action fighting Choctaws and Texans at a field called Massard Prairie, south of Fort Smith, Arkansas. Massard Prairie is not as famous as Shiloh. Neither is the Battle of Honey Springs, Indian Territory, as famous as the Battle of Gettysburg, Pennsylvania. Yet the men who died in the half-forgotten actions west of the Mississippi River sacrificed just as much as any who died in the famous, glorified battles in the East.

Thus this book is dedicated to my great-great-great-grandfather, Daniel Jennings, and others like him on both sides whose brave deeds and sacrifices in the war west of the Mississippi should not be forgotten.

KANSAS

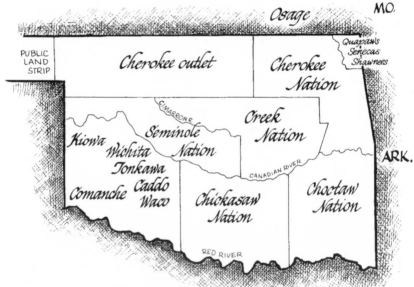

TEXAS

Contents

Foreword

Perhaps nowhere else than in Indian Territory did the term "brother against brother" truly epitomize the Civil War. The Five Civilized Tribes—Cherokee, Creek, Choctaw, Chickasaw, and Seminole—had been removed from their ancestral homes in the Southern states just over a quarter of a century earlier. The treaties associated with the removal created factions within each tribe. Feuds and vendettas were carried out for years until peace came to the Indian Nations in the form of prosperity. Large plantations, mercantile businesses, mills, successful family farms, schools, and churches marked the "golden age" in these tribes' new lands. Old grudges were soon put to rest.

The Kansas-Nebraska Act of 1854, however, interrupted that peace. The "squatter sovereignty" approach to lands bordering the Indian Nations, as well as Republican campaign overtures by William H. Seward in 1860 to seize the Indian lands and fill them with white settlers, stirred old political embers in the Five Civilized Tribes.

Tribal members became factional once again. Some members who wanted nothing to do with the states that had forced their removal spoke for loyalty to the United States or to the cause of abolition. Others aligned themselves with secessionists' strong economic ties to Southern banks and Southern lifestyles. Others tried to remain neutral.

Secessionists from Arkansas and Texas began courting the Indian Nations, while missionaries from Massachusetts and Pennsylvania encouraged loyalty to the United States. Outsiders, as well as the tribes themselves, began to recognize that their lands would soon become a buffer zone or a pass-through for warring armies if war erupted. The rivers and roads that promoted commerce would soon be occupied by refugees and men of war.

When war did erupt, loyal Unionist families fled to Kansas while secessionists fled to the Red River for safety. As the war progressed, old vendettas resurfaced; guerrilla tactics, murder, robbery, and property destruction were rampant. Families with ties to the Union were burned out and murdered by secessionists. Families with ties to the newly formed Confederacy were burned out and murdered by Unionists. The once prosperous Nations became a no-man's land. Crops, livestock, and businesses were in ruin.

At war's end, 14 percent of the Indian population in Indian Territory were orphans, another 16 percent were fatherless children, and 33 percent of the population were widows. The Five Tribes were more destitute than at the time of their removal.

While battles involving thousands of troops raged in the East in a gentleman's war, the conflict in Indian Territory saw families trapped in a vicious guerrilla-style war. This book provides an overview of the significant military actions in Indian Territory. At the same time it provides an insight into the impact of those engagements on the local population as well as the Trans-Mississippi Theater in the War Between the States.

WHIT EDWARDS
Director of Education
Oklahoma Historical Society

Acknowledgments

No man ever accomplished anything entirely by himself. Anyone who claims to have done so is a dang liar. When my artistic friend and fellow history buff, Andy Thomas, suggested that we work on a book together, it spurred me into action. The end result was *Civil War in the Indian Territory*. Thanks to Andy, this book (with its fine illustrations) is a reality. I would like to thank the staff of Wilson's Creek National Battlefield, particularly park rangers Jeff Patrick and Steve Weldon, for their help in obtaining excellent research material. Also I am grateful for the help I received from my great-uncle, Rex Lawson, who provided additional sources. A special thanks to Marlene Agan, whose skill on the word processor was invaluable. Of course, I am deeply indebted to the authors listed in this book's bibliography; they made this little volume possible. And last but not least, my wife Rhonda deserves honorable mention. Rhonda Rae has been living the last two decades of the twentieth century with a guy who spends a great deal of his spare time in the middle of the nineteenth century. For such a test of endurance, she has earned a special commendation for patience above and beyond the call of duty.

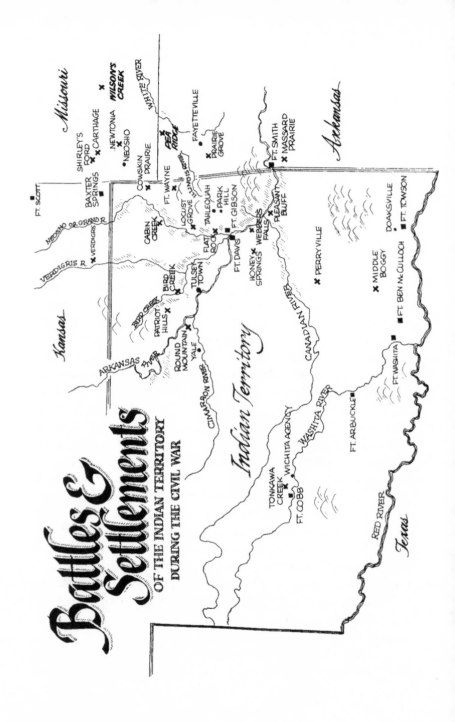

CHAPTER 1

Into the Valley of Death
1861

In the spring of 1861, America entered her most tragic and violent era. At the time, the land we know today as the state of Oklahoma was called the Indian Territory. It was home to a number of Native American tribes which had been displaced from their ancestral homelands by the government of the United States. Most people in the Territory belonged to what were known as the "Five Civilized Tribes." The Cherokee, Choctaw, Chickasaw, Creek, and Seminole people had their own sovereign nations in the Territory, ostensibly under the protection of the United States. As a matter of fact, the Territory was sometimes referred to as the "Indian Nations."

The question as to whether or not Native Americans would play a military role in the American Civil War was answered on a Missouri battlefield less than three weeks after the First Battle of Bull Run, Virginia. The Federal government's 1861 campaign to secure control of Missouri resulted in the bloody Battle of Wilson's Creek on August 10 near the town of Springfield in the southwest corner of the state. Conspicuous in the blazing action was a small force of Cherokee Indians led by Capt. Joel Mayes. Mayes was a well-known mixed-blood Cherokee cattle rancher who, years after the war, would become chief of his tribe. History has recorded only a few sketchy details about his unit at the Battle of Wilson's Creek. However, we do know that this single company of Native Americans, serving as scouts for Confederate brigadier general Ben McCulloch's army, was given credit by some sources of the time period for two critical actions which turned the tide of battle in favor of the South.

First, the Confederate warriors were said to have assisted in the dramatic charge by the 3rd Louisiana Infantry Regiment against the German-American troops of Union colonel Franz Sigel who had attacked the southern end of McCulloch's sprawling encampment. According to the accounts, the Cherokees were with the Southern troops who overran Sigel's artillery, capturing several cannons. Boldly, the small Indian force is said to have then moved rapidly through the clouds of sulfurous gunsmoke to the northern end of the battlefield. There the Union's main force, under Brig. Gen. Nathaniel Lyon, was desperately holding a rise of land which came to be known as Bloody Hill. General Lyon's hard-fisted surprise attack on the northern end of McCulloch's camp had been stalled on the hill by a thunderous Rebel artillery barrage. Although they held the high ground, the battered Yanks were vastly outnumbered and faced fierce assaults by overwhelming numbers of frenzied Southern troops. General Lyon rallied the 2nd Kansas Volunteer Infantry for a desperate counterattack. As the Kansas regiment marched across a stretch of open ground to prepare for the charge, a sudden burst of gunfire erupted at close range on the front of the column. Some sources claim this volley of musketry came from none other than the Cherokee company which had stealthily positioned itself within a thicket of brush close to the Union battle line. The surprising hail of deadly lead took its toll. Lyon himself was blown out of his saddle, becoming the first Union general to be killed in action during the Civil War. His successor continued the fruitless defense of the hill briefly, then retreated north.

The fearless men of Captain Mayes' company were among a growing number of new Confederate Cherokee recruits who rallied under Col. Stand Watie, a fiery leader within the tribe whose stubborn resistance to Federal troops during the war would become legendary. Watie was three-quarters Cherokee, although his appearance was more like that of a full-blood. Short and stocky, with legs bowed from years on horseback, this 55-year-old natural leader of men spoke little, but when he did, what he said was worth hearing. As early as July, Watie had established a military training camp at the site of an abandoned U.S. Army post named Fort Wayne, near present-day Watts, Oklahoma. With the official authorization of Gen. Ben McCulloch, he organized and trained an elite Indian regiment.

Early efforts by the Confederate government to win over the Five Civilized Tribes resulted in Stand Watie and a number of other influential Indian leaders casting their lot with the Southern Cause. The South's success in this endeavor was largely the result of the negotiating skills of its appointed representative, Commissioner Albert Pike. Pike was a huge, bear-like man with curly hair falling to his shoulders and a long, full beard. Originally from Boston, he was a journalist, scholar, and poet who opened a law practice in Arkansas. As a frontier lawyer, he represented Indians in court litigation and became experienced in dealing with their chiefs and councils. In May 1861, he set forth from Arkansas at the head of a long line of wagons loaded with potted food, wine, and other provisions for comfort in the wilderness, as well as various trade goods for the Indians. The wagon train lumbered off to Indian Territory as Pike sat comfortably in a buggy, armed with authorization from the Confederacy to spend $100,000 for treaties of alliance with the tribes of the region.

Pike's task was not as easy as he hoped it would be. Although the Choctaws and Chickasaws, whose lands bordered Texas, readily sided with the South, the other three tribes seemed as divided as their Caucasian counterparts. Despite the fact that the U.S. government had forced large numbers of Cherokee, Creek, and Seminole people westward to Indian Territory a generation earlier (with considerable loss of Indian lives during the hardships of the removal), there was nevertheless strong support for the Union among tribal factions. Even though the principal chief of the Cherokee, John Ross, was only one-eighth Indian and owned about 100 slaves who worked his vast plantation, he initially opposed alliance with the Confederacy. Likewise, the 80-year-old influential Creek chief Opothleyoholo stood firm in his conviction not to break his commitment of peace with the U.S. government. A pro-Union faction of the Seminole under Chief Billy Bowlegs opposed a pro-Confederate faction under John Jumper. Meanwhile, Stand Watie of the Cherokee Tribe and the wealthy, slave-owning Creek leaders, Daniel and Chilly McIntosh, along with Creek principal chief Motey Kennard, led a vigorous campaign of support for Pike's offers of Confederate alliance.

As a result of these political differences, old factional feuds within the tribes, dating from their forced removal, erupted once again. Three decades earlier, some Indian leaders had given in to the U.S. government by selling tribal lands and signing

away the land of their forefathers in the southeastern United States. Watie and the McIntosh brothers were among the members of these "Treaty Factions." Many who opposed the sale of Indian lands swore vengeance upon the members of the Treaty Factions and their families who swiftly moved west and settled in Indian Territory. Later when the vengeful tribal members were finally forced to relocate in the Territory themselves, they assassinated most of those who were the ringleaders in the sale of Indian land to the U.S. government. The old wounds from this inner-tribal conflict bled once again as Commissioner Pike found himself in the middle of a swirling storm of bitter feuds and political rivalries.

As the controversy raged over which side the "civilized" tribes would take in the war, Pike made sure he was leaving no loose ends elsewhere. Small groups of Quapaws, Senecas, and Shawnees in the northeast corner of the Territory would be no

Pike's wagon train lumbered off to Indian Territory.

problem if Stand Watie continued to exert his influence among his people, for the little bands were sure to follow the course of their powerful neighbors in the Cherokee Nation. However, other small tribes in the Territory needed special attention. Pike rode farther west to settle affairs with the "wild" tribes of the plains in Indian Territory. Escorted by Creek chief Kennard, Chilly McIntosh, Seminole leader John Jumper, and a mounted bodyguard of 60 Creek and Seminole warriors flying a Confederate flag, he met at the Wichita Agency near Fort Cobb with representatives of several tribes. Tonkawas, Caddos, and Wacos who had recently been removed from Texas to Indian Territory came to parley. Also Wichita tribal leaders and a large number of chiefs and headmen of the Comanche Tribe showed up. Pike treated the Indian leaders to feasts and presented them with guns and ammunition, saddles, hats, coffee, and tobacco. He also promised that the Confederacy would provide their tribes with an annual ration of food, livestock, tools, and other goods. In return, the chiefs put their marks on treaties of peace with the Confederate States of America. Unlike the agreements Pike was working on with the Five Civilized Tribes, the treaties signed at the Wichita Agency did not involve Indian military service. Although no commitments were made with the Kiowas, Pike's mission to the Plains Tribes in western Indian Territory was clearly a success. If he could succeed in the east as he had in the west, the Confederacy would control all of Indian Territory.

Finally a breakthrough came when Cherokee chief John Ross, at odds with his old political rival Stand Watie, gave in to those who urged him to sign Pike's alliance treaty. A cunning old politician, the 72-year-old Ross realized that a separate treaty between Colonel Watie and the Confederacy would strip him of his power as principal chief. He also knew that the millions of dollars still owed to his tribe by the United States for the "sale" of Cherokee lands in North Carolina, Georgia, and Tennessee was tied up in bonds issued in Southern states and would likely be nullified by the Federal government. However, Pike's treaty promised that the Confederacy would assume the

Federal government's financial obligations to the tribe and even seat a Cherokee delegate in the Confederate Congress in Richmond. Meanwhile, early impressive Confederate victories, first at Manassas, Virginia, then closer to home at Wilson's Creek, Missouri, convinced many Native Americans throughout the Territory that the Confederacy would prevail. They felt it would be in the best interest of all the tribes to be on the winning side.

Thus in early October, Pike was bound for home with a collection of signed documents that seemed to indicate his mission had been a huge success. Indeed Pike had done a good job, yet die-hard pro-Union leaders of the Creek and Seminole Tribes were still forces to be reckoned with. Also many Cherokee would prove to be less than firm in their loyalty to the South. The Confederacy had made serious commitments to the tribes in the treaty agreements, including the promise that Indian forces would not be called upon to fight unless their lands in the Territory were invaded. Should this promise be broken, the Confederacy could lose the trust of its Indian allies.

The Confederates had moved swiftly to consolidate their grip on Indian Territory. Texas troops had ridden into the region in April to capture forts Washita, Arbuckle, and Cobb without firing a shot. All three Federal posts had been abandoned and their small garrison forces recalled for service in the Eastern Theater of the war. All the Southern officers in the Territory were to cooperate with David Hubbard, the Confederate superintendent of Indian affairs, as the Confederate Congress had created a Bureau of Indian Affairs to be attached to the War Department. Stand Watie's regiment of mixed-blood Cherokees was the first Indian unit organized in the Territory. General Ben McCulloch, the victor of the Battle of Wilson's Creek, commissioned Watie a colonel in the Confederate Provisional Army. Meanwhile Chief John Ross had authorized the raising of another regiment of Cherokee troops, composed mainly of full-bloods who were political supporters of the chief, to be led by Col. John Drew, a loyal Ross follower. Drew's command was to be known as the 1st Regiment of Cherokee Mounted Rifles. Watie's unit was designated the 2nd Regiment of Cherokee Mounted Rifles. The two units had a very uneasy spirit of cooperation between them. Drew's men were mostly "pin Indians," politically opposed to Watie. Pins were members of a fraternal order within the Cherokee Tribe known as the Keetoowa Society, often referred to as the Pin Indian Organization. The members wore peculiar crossed pins, sometimes of feathers, and believed in preserving Cherokee independence, tribal customs, and traditions. Some of the older Pins had been among those who assassinated members of the Treaty Faction of the tribe; among their victims was Watie's half-brother, his uncle, and a cousin. Confederate Creek Indians were organized into the 1st Creek Cavalry Regiment led by their war chief, Col. Daniel McIntosh. His brother, Lt. Col. Chilly McIntosh, led a mixed unit of Creeks and Seminoles known as the 1st Seminole Cavalry Battalion with the Seminole Tribe's Confederate leader, Maj. John Jumper, second in command. Meanwhile, Choctaw and Chickasaw warriors were being trained and organized into the 1st Regiment of Choctaw and Chickasaw Mounted Rifles under Col. Douglas Cooper. Cooper was a white-bearded former U.S. Indian agent who, despite his fondness for liquor, was highly respected by the Choctaw Tribe, a people whom he honestly served before and after the war. A veteran of the Mexican War, he was the second ranking military officer in all Indian Territory. Overall command of Confederate Indian forces fell upon the shoulders of Albert Pike. Grateful for the success of his treaty mission, the Confederate government commissioned Pike a brigadier general and in November put him officially in charge of the Department of Indian Territory.

As General Pike prepared to leave on a trip to Richmond, Virginia, to oversee the ratification of his treaties and secure funds for equipping his Indian regiments, he received several disturbing reports of skirmishes between the Confederate and Union factions of the Creek Tribe. Before his departure, he sent orders to Colonel Cooper, his second in command, to restore peace among the Creeks. Cooper found the situation even worse than reported. Chief Opothleyoholo had gathered together thousands of his followers on his land near North Fork Town on the Canadian River, and small groups of his pro-Union warriors were already clashing with supporters of the McIntosh brothers. Cooper boldly rode into the Creek Nation with a small escort and received news that more than 3,500 Indians had joined the North Fork camp (some reports put the number as high as 6,000). Many were women, children, and the elderly, but Opothleyoholo could field a fighting force of about 1,500 men. Most, of course, were Creek warriors, but some were Seminoles who opposed Confederate major John Jumper's leadership and preferred instead to follow pro-Union leaders in the tribe such as the Seminole headman, Alligator. Also included in this force was a number of African-Americans who had escaped slavery and fled to Opothleyoholo's camp where they were welcomed and armed as fighting men. Muzzle-loading shotguns, hunting rifles, knives, and tomahawks were the most common weapons found in Opothleyoholo's camp. Such was the case in all Native-American military camps during the war in the Territory. Very few primitive weapons such as bows, spears, and war clubs were utilized.

Colonel Cooper sought unsuccessfully to arrange a meeting with Opothleyoholo and avoid open warfare with his people. The Creek chief would not even dignify his written requests with an answer. Cooper also received reports that the chief was communicating with Federal authorities in Kansas. As a matter of fact, Opothleyoholo had exchanged communiqués with E. H. Carruth, a U.S. Indian agent in Kansas, who encouraged the old chief to resist the Confederacy and promised that U.S. troops would soon cross into Indian Territory and crush all enemy forces. Cooper soon became concerned that if he hesitated to take action, Opothleyoholo might ally himself with Union forces from Kansas, and there would be the devil to pay. The hard-drinking colonel made an important command decision: he would retire to the Confederate post at Fort Gibson, consolidate his forces, and march against Opothleyoholo, "and either compel submission" to the Confederacy or "drive him and his party from the country."

Meanwhile, the huge herd of livestock at the North Fork camp had consumed the grass for miles around. It became apparent to Opothleyoholo that he must move his people, otherwise their livestock would starve. He decided to break camp and march to the northwest where grass would be plentiful, and he could be closer to the Kansas border where he believed Union reinforcements were gathering.

During their trek north through the cool autumn breeze, the Union Indians were accused by pro-Confederate Creeks of driving off their cattle, kidnapping women and children, and stealing more than 300 slaves. They were also said to have been reinforced by a band of "Jayhawkers" (Union raiders from Kansas). It was rumored that the Kansans had robbed several cabins and burned a trading post. Opothleyoholo replied that the cattle belonged to his people, the women and children followed of their own free will, and no Kansans had joined him.

By November 15, Colonel Cooper was ready to ride from Fort Gibson with a mounted force of 1,400 men. His motley little army included six companies of the 1st Choctaw and Chickasaw Mounted Rifles, the 1st Creek Cavalry Regiment, the 1st Seminole Cavalry Battalion, and 500 troopers of the 9th Texas Cavalry who had been assigned to support the Indians. Cooper's Native-American troops were self-supplied with shotguns and rifles they had brought from home along with their own ponies. Most wore civilian clothing of wool and cotton with trade blankets for warmth. A few wore buckskins, and some even painted their faces for war. Nearly all wore their hair in the traditional, shoulder-length fashion. As a matter of fact, they looked nearly identical to their foes in Opothleyoholo's quasi-military force.

Colonel Cooper rode out of Fort Gibson on November 15, confident that he would catch up with Opothleyoholo's force since it was encumbered with thousands of civilians with their

*Chief Opothleyoholo challenged
Confederate authority.*

ponderous baggage wagons, oxcarts, and herds of livestock. Toward the end of the first day's march, an abandoned camp of the Union Indians was found. From there the trail was followed until about four o'clock on the afternoon of November 19 when campfire smoke was spotted in the distance near the Red Fork of the Arkansas River. Cooper ordered Lt. Col. William Quayle, commander of the Texas battalion, to charge the camp. With a wild cheer the Texans surged forward, sweeping into the campsite only to find it deserted. Sizing up the situation, Lieutenant Colonel Quayle realized the site was merely an outpost and concluded that the main camp must be nearby. From high ground near the site, a group of Union Creek scouts surveyed the scene. Quayle decided to pursue them all the way to Opothleyoholo's camp. Spoiling for a fight, the Texas troopers thundered across the rolling prairie for several miles, chasing the Creeks until dusk to a site known as Round Mountain. There the reckless Rebel cavalrymen followed the scouts to a skirt of timber lining a stream and immediately received a devastating volley of gunfire. Quayle had indeed found Opothleyoholo's camp, and the wiley old chief was ready for him. Swirling clouds of gunsmoke rolled from the woods as men and horses struggled to break free from a deadly rain of bullets. Stunned and disorganized, the Texans beat a hasty retreat as the Creek warriors kept up a merciless rate of fire from behind the tree line. Then with war whoops, they rushed forward in pursuit of the fleeing cavalry.

At the first sound of distant gunfire, Colonel Cooper deployed his Choctaw and Chickasaw Mounted Rifles and advanced to support Colonel Quayle. Night had fallen by the time Cooper reached the scene of the action. In the chaotic darkness, it was hard to tell friend from foe. Fiery flashes from sporadic gunfire briefly lit up shadowy figures running to and fro. A group of horsemen approached to within about 60 yards of the Mounted Rifles, and Cooper's aide, Col. James Bourland, yelled out to them, inquiring if they were Texans. He was answered by the crack of a rifle, and both sides immediately opened fire. The brief but violent encounter ended when the Creek horsemen suddenly disappeared into the night. Meanwhile, Colonel Quayle rallied his cavalry, and a number of the Texas troopers rejoined the engagement, falling in with the Choctaws and Chickasaws.

Opothleyoholo realized that his position would soon be untenable if he continued to resist Cooper's combined units of well-drilled Texas cavalry and trained Indian troops at Round Mountain. Unlike Cooper's force, his men had never received any regular military training. As a diversion to cover their retreat, the Union Indians started a prairie fire beyond the right flank of the Confederate battle line, threatening Cooper's supply wagons. Breaking contact with their foes, Opothleyoholo's warriors joined their families already in flight, heading northeast. Fording the cold Arkansas River during the night, they headed for a village of Union-sympathizing Cherokees on Bird Creek. Thus they left the Creek Nation's borders and crossed over into the Cherokee Nation. Colonel Cooper, choosing to avoid further mass confusion, did not pursue them in the darkness.

In the morning, Cooper's troops entered Opothleyoholo's abandoned campsite. They found only a few sheep and oxen, several old horses, and some broken wagons. Partially consumed sacks of coffee, sugar, and other foodstuffs were scattered about; however, the Creek chief's people had escaped with most of their livestock and other possessions. Cooper reported his casualties in the skirmish, known as the Battle of Round Mountain (sometimes called the Battle of Red Forks), as six killed, four wounded, and one missing. Opothleyoholo left no record of his losses. Round Mountain, the first serious clash of the war in Indian Territory, took place near the present-day town of Yale, Oklahoma.

So it was that Colonel Cooper's first battle in his campaign against Opothleyoholo was an ineffectual brawl in the dark with his foe escaping almost perfectly intact. Then to complicate matters, Cooper received orders from Brig. Gen. Ben McCulloch to break off his pursuit of the old chief and march his force

*Former Indian agent turned
Confederate commander, Douglas Cooper*

east to the Arkansas border near Maysville by Stand Watie's camp at Fort Wayne. McCulloch was mustering all the troop strength he could in order to face an advancing Union army of 20,000 soldiers under the command of Maj. Gen. John C. Frémont. After a four-day march to Concharta where fresh supplies awaited his army, Cooper received another dispatch from McCulloch. The communiqué stated that the Union army had ceased its advance and was withdrawing north. Once again, Colonel Cooper was free to conduct his war against Opothleyoholo.

On the morning of November 29, Cooper's men rode out of their campsite, well rested, fed, and ready for action. Cooper's plan called for his troopers to move out in two columns in order to ensnare the Union Indians between two converging forces: a classic pincer movement. The colonel himself took one column, consisting of Native-American troops, on a road leading northwest toward Tulsey Town, the forerunner of present-day Tulsa. Reports from his scouts led Cooper to believe Opothleyoholo's force was encamped near the small town. One of his scouts was a mixed-blood Cherokee named Clem Rogers, who would later have a son destined to become the famous humorist and film star, Will Rogers.

The Confederates' second column was made up of the 9th Texas Cavalry under Col. William B. Sims and Lieutenant Colonel Quayle. Sims' orders were to rendezvous with the 1st Cherokee Mounted Rifles under Col. John Drew at a village known as Coody's Settlement. Drew's command had been posted at Coody's since being mustered into service. Now they were finally to see action.

Upon reaching Tulsey Town and setting up camp, Cooper had the opportunity to question a Confederate who had been held prisoner in Opothleyoholo's camp on Bird Creek until he managed to escape. The former prisoner described the location of the Union Indian camp, estimated their force of warriors as numbering 2,000, and stated that they planned to attack Cooper's army soon. Southern military plans suddenly changed as Cooper dispatched several staff officers with messages for

Sims and Drew. Unfortunately for the Confederates, the change in plans only created a more confusing situation. Although Sims' Texans successfully joined up with Cooper's column at the designated new rendezvous point, Drew's regiment marched to a point on Bird Creek due to a misunderstanding of orders. This placed the unlucky Cherokees only about six miles northeast of Opothleyoholo's huge camp, with reinforcements from Cooper and Sims more than 24 hours away. Suddenly, approximately 2,000 Union warriors were within easy striking distance of Drew's 480 Confederate Indian troops.

Drew surrounded his camp with a series of strong outposts to prevent a surprise attack, then he and his men dug in, nervously awaiting Cooper's arrival. If the Creek and Seminole warriors chose to attack before Confederate reinforcements arrived, they could easily overrun the outnumbered Cherokees. As a matter of fact, most of the full-blood Cherokees were opposed to making war on Opothleyoholo's people. Even when Cooper and Sims finally arrived at Bird Creek and camped about two miles from Drew, his men still remained uneasy and grumbled about the injustice of the Confederates' relentless pursuit of Opothleyoholo. The Cherokee colonel failed to realize the seriousness of his men's discontent until the eve of battle on the night of December 8. Stepping from his stove-heated officers' tent into the cold night air, Drew glanced around his camp and suddenly became aware of an unnatural stillness. Nearly all his men had deserted, slipping away into the darkness! Aghast, Drew called for his orderly, who was still present, and ordered him to saddle his horse. Gathering his few remaining men, who numbered about 60, the distraught colonel started for Cooper's camp. Suddenly he realized that he had abandoned his supply of ammunition, which could soon fall into enemy hands. Drew ordered several men to continue the ride to Cooper with news of the disaster while he and the others returned to frantically retrieve the ammunition wagons.

Colonel Cooper and his staff were sitting around their campfire when news of the Cherokee mass desertion reached them.

Angrily jumping to his feet, Cooper thundered for his drummer to beat the "long roll," a signal for all soldiers to immediately fall into formation under arms. Troops were deployed to cover all approaches to the main Confederate camp. Cooper ordered Colonel Quayle to take a squadron of his cavalry and occupy the abandoned Cherokee camp. The entire Confederate force nervously rested on their weapons throughout the night. The next morning, December 9, Cooper ordered Drew (who had returned with his ammunition wagons) to take his remaining Cherokees, along with a detachment of Texans and Choctaws, to retrieve whatever else he could from his deserted camp. Cooper no doubt regretted that Col. Stand Watie and his loyal Confederate Cherokees were not present on this expedition in place of Drew's rebellious troops. Watie's 2nd Cherokee Mounted Rifles were still posted at old Fort Wayne near the Arkansas border.

When Drew returned with his tents, wagons, horses, and equipage, Cooper broke camp. By the afternoon, advance Confederate scouts were skirmishing with their foes along Bird Creek. Suddenly, heavy gunfire erupted at the rear of the Confederate column. According to Opothleyoholo's plan, 200 warriors were to bluff an attack on Cooper's force and then fall back, leading the Confederates into the old chief's carefully chosen defensive position. Cooper's force turned to meet the rear attack, then pursued the small force of mounted tribesmen to Opothleyoholo's chosen site of battle. The Union warriors were strongly posted at a gorge of a bend in Bird Creek called Chusto-Talasah or Little High Shoals. Cooper left his supply wagons on the prairie with a guard of a hundred men and deployed his troops for an all-out assault. The Union Creeks, Seminoles, and African-Americans had been joined by a large number of Cherokee deserters from Colonel Drew's command who now aimed their rifles and shotguns at their former Confederate comrades.

For more than four hours both sides blasted away at each other from behind trees and rocks along the bend in the creek.

Fighting in the traditional Indian fashion, from behind cover, the warriors burned a great deal of gunpowder, but casualties were limited. It was like a tremendous turkey hunt with hundreds of heads popping up from time to time in the brush, each presenting a target for only a split second. Several sorties by both sides were attempted throughout the afternoon, but they had little effect. Near the end of the day a group of Opothleyoholo's Creek warriors, fearsome in their war paint, made a mad dash toward the Choctaw-Chickasaw regiment's horses. In typical cavalry fashion, one out of every four soldiers had been detailed to hold the regiment's horses when the unit dismounted to fight on foot in the brush along Bird Creek. Colonel Cooper, alerted of the warriors' charge, rushed a detachment of cavalry to the assistance of the horse-holders. The Creeks' attack was repulsed, but their charge had totally disorganized the Mounted Rifles Regiment. When word spread that the regiment's horses were in danger of being captured, most of the Choctaws and Chickasaws abandoned their positions along the creek and ran for their mounts. Losing a horse in a fight like this could cost a man his life, leaving him stranded on hostile ground. Confederate major Mitchell Leflore desperately attempted to rally the disorganized Indian troops, but the sun was setting before they could finally be redeployed on the field. At nightfall the gunfire fizzled out. Recalling his troopers, Colonel Cooper retired from the battlefield and camped for the night about five miles from Chusto-Talasah.

The next morning, December 10, Cooper ordered out a strong column to check the enemy position. The Confederates found that Opothleyoholo had abandoned Chusto-Talasah during the night. His force was nowhere to be seen, but scouts discovered that his trail led in a northwesterly direction. Cooper put a burial detail to work, interring the dead that had been left on the battlefield. Confederate casualties totaled 15 killed and 37 wounded. Opothleyoholo's losses, as usual, were not recorded. The Battle of Bird Creek, also known as Chusto-Talasah, was fought just north of present-day Tulsa.

Cooper's chief of ordnance discovered that the tremendous

amount of gunfire at Bird Creek had nearly exhausted his supply of ammunition. Thus the Confederates were forced to
return to Fort Gibson for fresh supplies. Worried about the
desertion of Drew's men and the possibility that it would lead
to more mass desertions and even a shift of loyalty toward the
Union across the entire Indian Territory, Cooper wrote to the
Confederate high command in Arkansas requesting reinforcements. General Ben McCulloch had left on a trip to Richmond
to report on military affairs and, in his absence, Col. James
McIntosh (no relation to the Creek leaders) was in command of
his army. McIntosh was a dashing West Point graduate who had
been commended for his bravery at the Battle of Wilson's
Creek. The young, black-bearded colonel agreed with Cooper
that there was a serious military threat to Confederate authority that needed to be eradicated immediately. A man of action,
McIntosh took to the field himself, leading a Confederate States
cavalry force of 1,600 troopers into Indian Territory. His column
consisted of seven companies of the 11th Texas, a battalion of
the 3rd Texas, Maj. John Whitfield's Texas Cavalry Battalion, a
battalion of the 2nd Arkansas Mounted Rifles, and Capt. H. S.
Bennett's Independent Company of Texas Cavalry.

McIntosh reached Fort Gibson where he and Cooper held a
council of war on the evening of December 20 to work out their
campaign plans. They decided to move out in two columns.
Cooper's force, reinforced by Whitfield's Texas Battalion, was to
ride up the north side of the Arkansas River and attempt to get
in the rear of the enemy position. According to the latest scouting reports reaching Fort Gibson, Opothleyoholo's camp was
located on Shoal Creek, a tributary of the Verdigris River. McIntosh's force of Texas and Arkansas cavalry (no Indian troops)
would move up the Verdigris, reaching a point east of the camp,
then swing west and make a direct strike. Because forage was
known to be scarce in the region, McIntosh and Cooper agreed
that their foe should be attacked on sight, without delay.

McIntosh saddled up 1,380 of his troops on December 22
and rode out of Fort Gibson at noon. The weather had turned
miserably cold. While military campaigns across the rest of the

continent had ground to a halt with soldiers on both sides in winter quarters, the war in Indian Territory was reaching its peak of ferocity for 1861. McIntosh's column forded the ice-cold waters of the Grand River and took the road leading up the east side of the Verdigris. By Christmas Day they had crossed the Verdigris, pushing westward as planned, yet they had seen very few Indians, and those warriors had remained far distant from the Southern soldiers.

As the bleakest of all Christmas Days in American history came to an end, McIntosh's men were busy pitching camp when about 200 mounted Native-American warriors suddenly appeared in the distance, about half a mile away. The young colonel ordered out one of his regiments and personally led a pursuit of the warriors. However, he soon came to the conclusion that he and his men were being led "on a fruitless chase" and ordered his troopers back to camp. This officer was too clever to fall for the same tricks used by the Union Indians at Round Mountain and Bird Creek. Indeed, Opothleyoholo and his people faced a force like no other they had encountered before. Not only was James McIntosh a clever, well-trained cavalry officer, but his men were real soldiers as well. They were tough frontier horsemen trained as regular Confederate cavalry. Many were hardened veterans of the Battle of Wilson's Creek. They spent Christmas evening in camp squaring away their gear and preparing their weapons for combat.

During the night a messenger arrived with a dispatch from Colonel Cooper. It stated that his progress on his route of march up the north side of the Arkansas River had been delayed by the desertion of a large number of his teamsters. Cooper estimated that it would be two or three days before his column could be in position to support McIntosh's cavalry as planned. After reading the dispatch, Colonel McIntosh boldly decided to press on without waiting for Cooper's Indian troops. He would have preferred to have their help, but he also felt their presence was not necessary for victory. His cavalry regulars could take on Opothleyoholo's tribesmen alone. Suddenly the war in the Territory had taken on the appearance of a classic confrontation between white cavalry troopers and Native-American warriors.

On the bitterly cold morning of December 26, Colonel McIntosh's horse soldiers rode steadily west toward Shoal Creek and the region known as Patriot Hills or Chustenahlah. Their equestrian march was cautious, with scouts thrown out in all directions, alert for hostile Indians. Meanwhile, by noon Opothleyoholo's warriors were ready for battle. His scouts had observed the cavalry's route of march, and now the Creeks crouched behind a heavy growth of blackjack trees on a steep, rocky hill overlooking Shoal Creek. The Seminole war chief, Halek Tustenuggee, had deployed his warriors along the slopes of the hill, which also had an excellent cover of trees and rocks with a fine view of the creek.

As the vanguard of McIntosh's column splashed across the icy waters of Shoal Creek, gunfire erupted from the rocky ridge before them. The hardy Texans jumped from their horses and ran for cover, immediately returning fire. When his main force of cavalry arrived on the scene, Colonel McIntosh deployed his troopers for a concentrated assault upon the ridge, which stood in front of them across 250 yards of open ground. He gave the order to attack, and the brassy echo of a bugle sounded the charge. Hundreds of war horses pounded madly through the water and across the prairie toward the hillside, which was soon enveloped in clouds of gunsmoke. In his report of the battle, McIntosh later described how his men bravely assaulted the hill "and rushed over its rugged side with the irresistible force of a tornado, and swept everything before it." Suddenly Opothleyoholo's warriors were running for their lives, relentlessly pursued by their foes across five or six other rocky ridges. Three times the Indians attempted to make a stand, with warriors taking cover behind boulders, only to have their resistance crushed by the onrushing Confederate juggernaut. Three miles from where the battle began, the remnants of Opothleyoholo's force gathered for a desperate last stand. Once more the cavalry seemed invincible as it smashed all remaining hope for the Native Americans in another devastating charge. Many fleeing tribesmen were pursued like wild animals and shot down in their tracks until about an hour before sunset when the bugles finally sounded recall.

Colonel McIntosh reported his casualties in the Battle of Chustenahlah, also known as Patriot Hills, as only three dead and 32 wounded. He estimated Opothleyoholo's killed as "upwards of 250." The Confederates captured 160 women and children, 20 African-Americans, 30 wagons, 70 yoke of oxen, about 500 horses, several head of cattle, 100 sheep, and interestingly, thousands of dogs (an important part of the Indian food supply). No warriors were listed as being taken alive. In the abandoned Indian camp, the soldiers found hundreds of buffalo robes and great quantities of foodstuffs. Many beads and trinkets were kept as trophies by the victorious cavalrymen. One very notable souvenir was found by a Texan: a silver medal, dated 1694, commemorating a peace treaty between the Creek Tribe and the British government.

Gathering together the survivors of the day's horrendous disaster, Opothleyoholo immediately set out for Kansas. His people had been forced to abandon much of what they needed for survival. The long, cold trek which now faced them would be worse than anything they had yet endured.

At daybreak on December 27, McIntosh's men were already in the saddle. In the vanguard of their column was none other than Col. Stand Watie and his 2nd Cherokee Mounted Rifles. Watie's 300 Cherokee troopers had reached the battlefield the day before just as the last shots were fired and now, anxious to prove their prowess in battle, they spearheaded the pursuit of Opothleyoholo. Colonel Douglas Cooper, still attempting to catch up with McIntosh, had issued orders to Watie on December 23 to rendezvous with McIntosh's cavalry as soon as possible.

The Confederate column soon found Opothleyoholo's trail and, after riding about 25 miles, sighted two wagons. To prevent their capture, the teamsters cut loose their teams and hastily set the wagons afire. Soon afterward, McIntosh heard gunfire in

The brassy echo of a bugle sounded the charge.

the distance, and a hard-riding courier informed him that Watie had located a sizable enemy force. After a quick survey of the enemy position, the tough little Cherokee colonel had divided his force. Watie sent half his regiment under Maj. Elias Boudinot to the left of their foe, while he led the rest on a strike against the right flank of the Union Indians who had taken cover in a series of gorges. It was rough terrain, defended by desperate warriors, but after an hour and a half of blazing action, the exhausted Creeks and Seminoles abandoned their rocky defenses and continued their retreat. In this unnamed, nearly forgotten skirmish, Watie's men counted the bodies of 11 Union dead left on the field while they themselves did not lose a man. They also captured 75 women and children and about 30 pack horses.

While camping on Shoal Creek the night of December 27, Colonel McIntosh decided that he had accomplished his mission. Opothleyoholo's rebellion against the Confederacy had been crushed, and the old chief was no longer a threat to Southern authority. His people were scattered across the countryside, struggling through the sleet and snow toward Kansas. The next morning, McIntosh broke camp and set out for Fort Gibson. From there, after being resupplied, he and his men would return to Arkansas.

Meanwhile, Colonel Cooper's force had pushed on north. Sweeping through the region on a forced reconnaissance with limited provisions, Cooper's Native American troopers and Texas cavalry hounded the miserable Union Indians. In his report of this merciless expedition, Cooper stated that his force killed six of the enemy and captured 150. None of his own men were battle casualties; however, the weather was so severe, one of the Confederate troopers froze to death. Thus the terrible saga of Opothleyoholo's Revolt came to an end as the suffering survivors crossed the border into Kansas. Freezing weather and disease continued to claim countless Indian lives as they huddled together in squalid refugee camps, praying for an early spring and swift vengeance on their oppressors.

CHAPTER 2

Blood and Fury
1862

Brigadier General Albert Pike returned to Indian Territory in February of 1862. During that critical time, the wintering Confederate forces in southern Missouri and northern Arkansas found their training for the oncoming spring campaign season rudely interrupted. An army of 12,000 Union troops was marching south with the intention of decisively crushing Confederate military power in the region.

Major General Earl Van Dorn, newly appointed commander of the Confederate Trans-Mississippi District, sent word to General Pike to march his Native American troops to Arkansas and join his "Army of the West." Pike was not pleased. The treaties on which he labored so hard specifically stated that Indian forces would not be required to fight outside their Territory. Yet obviously the impending showdown between the two largest armies west of the Mississippi River was going to profoundly affect the future of Indian Territory. Reluctantly, Pike prepared to carry out his orders as a good soldier should. However, his 1st Creek Cavalry Regiment and 1st Seminole Cavalry Battalion refused to leave the Territory until the Confederacy paid overdue treaty payments. Wisely, Pike did not press the issue and left the Territory without his Creeks and Seminoles. He entered Arkansas with 800 men of the 1st and 2nd Cherokee Mounted Rifles (the 1st Regiment had been reorganized

Gen. Albert Pike

with Colonel Drew still in command). Pike was also accompanied by an independent unit of 200 white troopers known as Welch's Texas Cavalry, giving him a total command in Arkansas of 1,000 men. Still plagued with logistical problems, Colonel Cooper's 1st Choctaw and Chickasaw Mounted Rifles once again lagged far behind, destined to miss the great battle. Cooper's men managed to approach within earshot as the last guns were fired at a place known as Pea Ridge.

It was a clash of arms unlike any the Native American troops would ever experience again. As ominous gray clouds spit snow down upon that field in Arkansas, more than 25,000 men fought for two days in the most decisive battle west of the Mississippi. On March 7-8, 1862, the two armies hammered away at each other in a deadly firestorm of musketry and cannon fire that left more than 2,400 casualties.

For their part, Pike's Indians brought a brief success to Confederate efforts on the first day of battle. They were deployed near a village called Leetown, west of the huge, pea vine-covered ridge for which the battle was named. With the assistance of their Texas allies, the Cherokees launched a fierce charge across an open field, driving back five companies of Federal cavalry and capturing three artillery pieces. However, immediately after their dramatic assault, the jubilant warriors held a premature victory celebration, losing their discipline around the captured gun battery. When their blue-coated foes began shelling the position, Pike's men scrambled for cover, retreating pell-mell to the safety of nearby woods. Advancing Union troops reported the discovery of a number of scalped casualties on this portion of the battlefield, which later caused a furor of outrage in the North over the conduct of Pike's Indian force. For the remainder of the battle, the Cherokees' participation was mainly limited to scouting and patrolling.

The Battle of Pea Ridge, or Elkhorn Tavern as it was known to the Confederates, was a disastrous defeat for the Southern Cause in the West. Pike and his Cherokees were not the only Confederates to experience a run of bad luck on that bloody field in Arkansas. Three Confederate generals, including Ben McCulloch and Opothleyoholo's nemesis, James McIntosh, fell with mortal wounds on the first day of battle. To top off the day's Southern disasters, the commander of the 3rd Louisiana Regiment was captured as his men, heroes of Wilson's Creek, were put to flight near Leetown, which burned to the ground during the night. On the second day of action, the battle centered around an inn called Elkhorn Tavern in the shadow of the imposing land mass known as Pea Ridge. On the first day, the Confederates had been successful near the tavern, but on the second, they found themselves running low on ammunition. Ironically, Van Dorn himself insured the defeat of his own army by failing to bring his supply wagons with him the previous day. Thus the Confederates were finally forced to retreat as they ran out of ammunition.

Van Dorn refused even to acknowledge Pike and his command in his official report of the battle. He verbally criticized the long-haired lawyer for losing control of his Indian troops after their capture of the Union artillery and looked down on them as savages who scalped and mutilated enemy dead. He and some of his fellow officers exaggerated the role which the Cherokee withdrawal had on the outcome of the battle. Incidentally, Van Dorn had made a name for himself before the war as an Indian fighter, leading U.S. cavalry against Comanches in Texas. Needless to say, he was not an admirer of Native American culture. Disillusioned, Pike marched back to Indian Territory. He had not wanted to break treaty agreements by taking his troops to Arkansas in the first place. Now he and his men found themselves ridiculed not only by their Union enemies, but by their fellow Confederates as well. It was a heavy price to pay for one brief moment of fleeting glory in an epic, historical battle.

After Pea Ridge, Van Dorn's Army of the West was transferred east of the Mississippi. Pike was outraged and viewed this action as another broken promise by the Confederate government, which had pledged to protect the tribes who signed the treaties of alliance. Also numerous arms and equipment that Pike had

The fierce Cherokee warriors charged their blue-coated foes.

ordered for his regiments had been commandeered by Van Dorn for use by his white troops. Pike became bitter and chose to ignore future orders from any high-ranking Confederate officers except from the very top levels of the government in Richmond itself. He had become a rebel among Rebels: an independent leader accountable to nearly no one but himself, setting up his own little Confederacy in Indian Territory.

General Pike developed his own strategy for the defense of the Territory. He believed his forces were too weak to defend the northern portion of the region, yet he felt a Union invasion was imminent. Since he knew the odds were against him, he wanted to make the invaders' march long and costly. Pike chose to withdraw south near the safety of the Texas border. In the Choctaw Nation, just north of the Red River, he built a stronghold on top of a hill on the prairie and named it Fort McCulloch, in honor of the deceased general. He directed his Creek and Seminole troops to stand guard over their own nations while Watie and Drew were to act as the advance guard, watching over the Cherokee lands bordering Kansas, Missouri, and Arkansas. Meanwhile at Fort McCulloch, Pike had additional forces at his disposal—a limited number of Arkansas infantry, artillery, and Texas cavalry that Van Dorn had left behind to face the overwhelming odds.

General Pike's concern over a Federal invasion of Indian Territory soon proved to be well-founded. By the end of spring, Kansas was desperate to rid itself of the thousands of starving Native Americans who had fled to the crowded refugee camps within its borders. These suffering victims of war's cruelty cried out for help to return to their homes, and many of them were willing to serve as soldiers to do so. Thus an invasion of Indian Territory by a Federal army, including two new regiments of Union Indian troops, was planned. The primary objective of this campaign, which came to be known as the Indian Expedition, was to escort the displaced Indians back to their homes while securing the Territory for the Union. Colonel William Weer of the 10th Kansas Infantry was chosen to command the expedition. The colonel's superior, Brig. Gen. James G. Blunt whose headquarters was at Fort Leavenworth, had chosen Weer largely for political, rather than military, reasons. Like Blunt, Weer was a member of the radical circle of Kansas abolitionists who supported Sen. James Lane and his strong-arm tactics against slaveholders. Unfortunately, Weer was an unpredictable, sometimes cantankerous, heavy drinker.

Colonel Weer was authorized to enlist two Indian regiments for the expedition. To bolster the strength of these units, Weer also had under his command two regiments of white infantry along with three regiments of cavalry and two batteries of artillery. Weer began moving between LeRoy, Kansas, and the Osage Catholic Mission on the Neosho River, recruiting as many Native Americans as he could. Meanwhile, Weer's white troops were stationed at Fort Scott, Kansas, under Col. Charles Doubleday of the 2nd Ohio Cavalry. Spoiling for a fight, Doubleday and his men marched out of Fort Scott on June 1 without Weer and his Indian recruits. A few days later Doubleday had crossed the border into Indian Territory with the 2nd Ohio Cavalry, three companies of the 6th Kansas Cavalry, four companies of the 10th Kansas Infantry, the 9th Wisconsin Infantry, and the 2nd Indiana Artillery. Altogether, his force totaled about 2,500 men, each of whom was anxious to single-handedly whip all the "Johnny Rebs" in the entire Confederacy.

On June 6, Doubleday received a report of a Rebel camp on Cowskin Prairie, an area which extended east from Grand River along the Missouri-Arkansas border. The colonel took a detachment of about 1,000 troops, including infantry, cavalry, and artillery, and marched to the vicinity of Round Grove on Cowskin Prairie. It was sundown before the Confederate camp was finally located. Nightfall made the deployment of troops more difficult than usual, but it aided in a complete surprise of the enemy. Forming his troops in line of battle near the Confederate camp, Doubleday opened fire with his artillery. Suddenly, quiet campground scenes exploded in blinding thunderbolt flashes that showered the prairie with bivouac debris. Terrified

Southern troops dropped their meager dinner rations and scrambled desperately for the shelter of ravines. Soon the stern, threatening beat of military drums in the dark distance told them that a large force of Union infantry was advancing. The Confederate commander, none other than Col. Stand Watie himself, was unable to rally his frantic men who had been camping with a force of Missouri cavalry under Col. John T. Coffee. Bullets began to zip through the night air as the disorganized Confederates fled from the field, firing only a few parting shots that flew wild in the general direction of their foe. Around 9:00 P.M. the action was over. In one sense, it had been the best of all Civil War battles: no casualties were reported by either side. The morale of the Union troops soared as they learned that the force they had just whipped without losing a man was Watie's Cherokee Mounted Rifles, considered the best Confederate Indian unit in the entire Territory. But the action also served to give an early warning to the Confederates of the Federal invasion of Indian Territory.

After the action at Cowskin Prairie, a courier arrived in Doubleday's camp with orders from Colonel Weer. The communiqué stated that Doubleday was to rendezvous with Weer and his Indian regiments at Baxter Springs where a Union post had been established across the Kansas border. Weer stated, "I deem it not in consonance with the purpose of the expedition to advance far without the Indians." Thus Doubleday withdrew from Indian Territory and marched his troops back across the border as directed.

Meanwhile, Colonel Weer had been undergoing the most frustrating challenge of his military career in his attempt to recruit and train his two Indian regiments. The volunteers were not used to the white man's style of military discipline. For one thing, there was considerable confusion among the new recruits as to whose orders they should obey: their chiefs or their new unit officers. The first regiment, under the command of Col. Robert W. Furnas, was designated the 1st Indian Home Guard. It was composed of Creeks and Seminoles who had fought under Chief Opothleyoholo the previous winter. The second regiment, commanded by Col. John Ritchie, was designated the 2nd Indian Home Guard and was made up of miscellaneous tribesmen recruited at various reservations and refugee camps in Kansas. Its members included Cherokees, Delawares, Osages, Quapaws, Caddos, Shawnees, Kansa Indians, and Kickapoos. Weer's column covered about 10 miles a day. His Indian regiments made a picturesque sight on the march in their new, ill-fitting, blue uniforms astride their short Indian ponies with their long rifles across the pommels of their saddles. Each morning, as the column moved out, "war-whoops" were sounded up and down the line as the blue-coated warriors rode toward Baxter Springs with their families trailing along behind them, hoping to soon reclaim their homes.

Down in Indian Territory, the Confederate Cherokees sent urgent demands for help. Chief John Ross was unsuccessful in his attempt to persuade General Pike to leave his defensive

*With their families trailing along
behind them, the blue-coated warriors rode south.*

position at Fort McCulloch and march north to meet the oncoming Federal invasion. Therefore, Stand Watie and John Drew appealed to the Confederate high command in Arkansas for reinforcements. At that time, a new Confederate commander, Maj. Gen. Thomas Hindman, was preoccupied with rebuilding Confederate strength in Arkansas through the use of forced conscription. Hindman could spare no men; as a matter of fact, he had ordered Pike to send all his white troops to Little Rock. He further directed Pike to lead his Indian forces north to reinforce Watie and Drew. However, Pike preferred to adhere to his own strategy and at first refused to obey Hindman's orders. Later, he partially complied and sent Colonel Cooper and several companies of his Choctaws and Chickasaws north, while he dispatched some Arkansas infantry and artillery to Little Rock. However, both detachments were slow in arriving at their destinations, and Hindman concluded that the stubborn General Pike would never comply with his orders. Thus the exasperated Hindman finally sent a battalion of Missouri cavalry under Col. J. J. Clarkson to defend the Cherokee Nation and, if possible, raid southern Kansas.

On June 28, Colonel Weer's combined forces of white and Indian troops, totaling 6,000, marched out of Baxter Springs. Entering Indian Territory in two columns, Weer's troops made short work of the outnumbered Confederates. July 3 became a fateful day of combat as the 6th Kansas Cavalry surprised Col. Stand Watie's regiment near Spavinaw Creek. A desperate running fight ensued as hundreds of horses galloped across the hot, dry prairie. Gunsmoke mingled with clouds of dust as Watie's men finally scattered in a typical guerrilla style, breaking up into small groups to prevent their pursuers from overtaking their entire force. The same day, the 9th Kansas Cavalry and the 1st Indian Home Guard reached Colonel Clarkson's camp just before sunrise at the village of Locust Grove. Silently, they surrounded the Confederate bivouac and took aim at the tents and blankets scattered about the grounds. The morning silence was shattered by unnerving blasts of gunfire as the camp erupted in panic and chaos. Scouts had led Clarkson to believe there were no Union troops nearer than the Grand River. Now his Missouri troopers were caught in a deadly storm of flying lead as the wrath of the Federal government rained down upon them. Colonel Clarkson, in his nightshirt, soon surrendered 110 half-clothed and confused Confederate survivors. Those who had escaped through the brush when the first shots rang out fled to Tahlequah, spreading more panic. Once again, most of Colonel Drew's Pin Cherokees defected to the Union side when they learned of Clarkson's surrender at Locust Grove. These new Union recruits, many of whom had fought at the Battle of Pea Ridge for the Confederacy, gave Colonel Weer enough additional Native American troops to form a third Indian regiment, to be commanded by Col. William A. Phillips.

The next day, July 4, there was a jubilant Independence Day celebration in Weer's camp along Cabin Creek. No one had expected such a swift and nearly bloodless series of Union victories: Cowskin Prairie, Spavinaw Creek, and Locust Grove. A "grand review" parade was held by the troops as the new Indian recruits looked on in amazement at the military might and glory of the U.S. government. Later, in camp, the conquering heroes lifted their tin cups in numerous toasts to one another's bravery and boasted of their plans for total victory in Indian Territory. Weer's little army seemed invincible that sunny day as his artillery fired a roaring salute to the Fourth of July, 1862.

On July 10, Colonel Weer marched his command farther south and set up camp on Flat Rock Creek near Grand River, 18 miles north of Confederate-held Fort Gibson. Weer then sent a detachment of cavalry to take Tahlequah, the capital of the Cherokee Nation, and arrest Principal Chief John Ross. Captain Harris Greeno led one company of the 6th Kansas Cavalry and about 50 Indian soldiers east to the Cherokee town. Greeno deployed his troops to surround the village but soon discovered there was not a single man left in the community. Thus Greeno and his men triumphantly entered Tahlequah, capturing the Cherokee capital without firing a shot. Next, Greeno headed southeast and found the principal chief at Park Hill, several miles outside Tahlequah, where John Ross' spacious plantation was located. About 200 troopers of Colonel Drew's 1st Cherokee Mounted Rifles surrendered with their chief and immediately volunteered to serve in Weer's Union force. As for the wily old politician Ross, he lost no time in pointing out that his alliance with the Confederacy was due merely to circumstances beyond his control. He was soon paroled and allowed to remain at his Park Hill mansion.

While Captain Greeno was capturing Tahlequah and Chief Ross, another Union detachment was marching to the vicinity of Fort Gibson and the Arkansas River. About 800 troopers rode out of the Flat Rock camp accompanied by Colonel Weer himself. Soon into the march, the cavalrymen became anxious to reach the cool, flowing water of the Arkansas River. The weather had been bone dry, and the heat was sweltering. All the creeks in the region had rapidly shrunk into isolated ponds of stagnant water. Away from their base camp near Grand River, Weer's troops had to rely on the filthy little pools that remained in the creek beds. Frequently, cattle stood in the ponds, seeking relief from the heat and flies. Such water had to be skimmed, boiled, and then spiked heavily with coffee before it was barely tolerable for drinking.

The vanguard of Weer's reconnaissance force saw some light action near Fort Gibson where they briefly skirmished with Confederate pickets guarding the outskirts of the post. When Weer's full detachment reached the Arkansas River three miles farther south of the fort, they discovered to their dismay that Col. Douglas Cooper's Choctaws and Chickasaws were already camped there on the opposite side of the stream. The two sides briefly traded shots along the riverbank before the Union troops withdrew, heading back to their base camp. Upon reaching Flat Rock, Colonel Weer retired to his tent with a good supply of whiskey and spent the better part of the next ten days incapacitated and apparently unconcerned with the rapidly deteriorating conditions in camp. Supply wagons from

Chief John Ross

Fort Scott, Kansas, were long overdue, and reports of increased Confederate guerrilla activity north of Flat Rock were alarming. Stand Watie's force had regrouped and remained a constant threat to the Union supply line. Military discipline fell apart. Hungry Native American troops left camp on lengthy hunting trips and frequently failed to return. The white troops, surviving on half rations, grumbled about their drunken commander and seriously considered mutiny. What had started out as a splendid campaign on the march to total victory had suddenly decayed into a disastrous expedition on a dead-end road to defeat. Finally, a group of officers, led by Col. Frederick Salomon of the 9th Wisconsin Volunteers, stomped across the miserable encampment toward Weer's tent and placed their inebriated leader under arrest. Salomon, a former Prussian Army officer, had commanded German-American troops in Missouri battles at Carthage and Wilson's Creek. Now he was in command of a mutinous Union army in Indian Territory, apparently cut off from its supply line and slowly becoming encircled by enemy forces.

Colonel Salomon sent word to his superior, General Blunt at Fort Leavenworth, of the drastic measures he and his fellow officers had taken against Weer. He then made preparations to march his miserable troops back to Kansas and ordered the three Indian regiments and one section of Kansas artillery to remain behind in the Territory to resist Cooper, Watie, and various guerrilla bands in the region. He also sent a detachment to Park Hill to once again take Chief Ross into custody. The chief was allowed to ride in a carriage with his family, along with about a dozen wagons loaded down with Ross' personal possessions as well as the archives and treasury of the Cherokee Nation. Thus he accompanied the Union army back to Kansas, leaving the Indian Territory and Cherokee nation behind him. He was destined never to return. Eventually, Ross was allowed to travel to Washington, D.C., to explain his situation to President Abraham Lincoln but found little sympathy. Ross died in Washington in 1866, protesting to the end that the abandonment of the Territory in 1861 by Federal troops had forced him to sign a treaty with the Confederacy.

When Colonel Salomon finally reached Fort Scott, Kansas, with his hard-worn veterans of the Indian Expedition, he faced an irate General Blunt who did not at all approve of his withdrawal from the Territory. There was even some talk of court-martial proceedings for both Salomon and Weer, but nothing ever became of it because, as Blunt explained, "an investigation would consume more time than could be afforded." Instead, Blunt reorganized his army and began formulating plans for another invasion of Indian Territory, this time with himself personally at the head of his troops in the field. Instead of being court-martialled, Salomon was promoted to brigadier general and placed in charge of a brigade in Blunt's force while, amazingly, Colonel Weer was also given command of a brigade as if nothing troublesome had ever happened! No doubt Weer's political connections served him well.

Meanwhile down in Indian Territory, a reign of terror had erupted with the departure of the main Union army. Innertribal warfare reached a bloody peak of ferocity, especially in the Cherokee Nation. Homes were burned, crops destroyed, livestock slaughtered, and unarmed men were gunned down for their political beliefs. After briefly occupying Fort Gibson and skirmishing with Watie's men, the three Union Indian regiments that Salomon had left behind also withdrew from the Territory along with the unlucky Kansas artillerymen assigned to assist them. Most of the Union Indian families who had tried to regain their homes now fled back to Kansas to once more endure the misery of the refugee camps. Thus the Indian Territory was again left in Confederate hands as victorious Cherokee Rebels named Stand Watie as their new principal chief.

Far to the south, still brooding behind the defenses of Fort McCulloch, Gen. Albert Pike received a dispatch from Fort Smith, Arkansas. Major General Thomas Hindman was ordering Pike to once again march his forces to Arkansas, this time to join the new Confederate army which was being assembled at

Fort Smith to attempt an invasion of Union-held Missouri. For Pike, this was the last straw. Outraged, he resigned his officer's commission and issued a farewell message to his Native American troops that included a scathing criticism of the Confederate government. After reading Pike's controversial treatise, Col. Douglas Cooper accused him of being either "insane or a traitor." General Hindman was also offended and wrote to Richmond requesting that the War Department disapprove Pike's resignation so that he could receive a military court-martial instead. A detachment of Confederate cavalry was sent to Fort McCulloch to take Pike into custody, and he was escorted without incident to Little Rock. However, the court-martial never took place as word soon reached Confederate headquarters in Arkansas that Pike's resignation had been accepted. So it was that Albert Pike simply walked away from the war into the shadows of history, declaring that he had never wanted "the damned command" in the first place.

Assuming command of all Confederate Native American troops, Colonel Cooper promptly complied with General Hindman's request for reinforcements from Indian Territory. Cooper crossed the border into Arkansas with his Choctaws and Chickasaws, about 200 Texas cavalrymen, and Colonel Watie's Cherokees—a combined force of about 2,000 troops. No longer plagued with logistical delays, Cooper then rode into Missouri in advance of Hindman's main army which still remained in Arkansas. Near the village of Newtonia, Cooper joined forces with about 2,300 other hard-riding troopers under the command of Col. Joseph O. "Jo" Shelby. Six artillery pieces added additional strength to the Southern forces camped around the village.

Sporadic skirmishing with Union troops in the vicinity had already taken place before Cooper's arrival. The Union commander of the district, Gen. John M. Schofield, had been alerted of the Confederate build-up near Newtonia and was gathering all the available Federal forces in the area, including that of General Blunt, to once again drive the Rebels from the state. A couple of preliminary skirmishes had involved some of Blunt's Union Indian troops, members of Colonel Ritchie's 2nd Indian Home Guard, who had advanced into the region by early September.

Early in the morning on September 14, 1862, a strong detachment of Colonel Shelby's 5th Missouri Cavalry Regiment, under the command of Capt. Ben Elliott, surrounded a camp of approximately 250 Native Americans and runaway slaves near the town of Carthage, county seat of Jasper County, Missouri. Citizens of the town had sent a plea for help to Shelby's camp. The Indians had reportedly been terrorizing the town, robbing and burning homes indiscriminately. The 2nd Indian Home Guard had indeed already established an infamous reputation for a severe lack of discipline and tended to pillage and plunder wherever they went. Among the most feared members of the regiment were the Osage warriors. Unlike members of the other tribes serving in the Union Army, the Osage continued to pluck the hair from their heads in the old fashion, leaving only a scalp lock down the center. They were very fearsome in both their appearance and in their manner of dealing with anyone who opposed them. Not only did they take scalps as trophies from their foes, but it was also their custom to decapitate their victims as well. They still adhered to many of their old, primitive tribal ways at this time in their history and simply did not conform well to the white man's style of military life.

When his men charged the Indian camp, Captain Elliott encountered very little resistance as the surprised tribesmen and their allies scrambled desperately for cover. For two hours the Missouri cavalrymen mercilessly hunted their prey through the woods and brush near Carthage. The band was entirely dispersed, with many gunned down in their tracks. About 200 new rifles that had been issued to them at Fort Scott were captured.

Six days later, on September 20, the main camp of the 2nd Indian Home Guard was the target of a surprise attack by the 31st Texas Cavalry under Col. T. C. Hawpe and a unit of local guerrillas under Maj. Tom Livingston. The action took place northwest of Carthage along Spring River at a crossing in the stream known as Shirley's Ford. As the Confederates opened their assault on Colonel Ritchie's camp, a stampede of hundreds of women and children took place. Ritchie's regiment lived like a nomadic tribe, carrying along the wives and children of its men. At first the motley Union warriors were driven back, but they soon rallied and stubbornly traded volleys with their assailants. An attempt to surround the Yankee tribesmen was unsuccessful, and Colonel Hawpe launched a series of dramatic but futile cavalry charges against them. Livingston then suggested to Hawpe that they concentrate on cutting off the Union supply wagons which he felt were vulnerable, but the colonel disagreed. A heated argument between the two resulted in an angry Hawpe withdrawing his troops from the field, leaving the defiant partisan leader and his men to take on the hundreds of frenzied warriors alone. Fighting desperately for their lives, Livingston and his surviving men successfully escaped with their scalps still attached to their skulls.

In his official report of the action at Shirley's Ford, Colonel Ritchie was unable to record exactly how many men he had lost, listing his casualties as anywhere from 12 to 20 killed and 9 wounded. He recorded the Confederate casualties as 22 killed. During the course of the day's action, Ritchie's men executed at least five citizen prisoners they had captured from the vicinity. Two of these victims were later discovered to be loyal Union men. This incident, coupled with the fact that several of the homes plundered by his regiment belonged to soldiers in Colonel Weer's regiment, led to Ritchie being relieved of command and subsequently placed under arrest. His regiment was entirely reorganized, with some of its most unruly members, including all the Osage warriors, being permanently discharged from Federal service.

By September 29, approximately 6,000 Union troops with 18 pieces of artillery were encamped 12 miles north of Newtonia at the town of Sarcoxie. Blunt's two brigades under Brigadier General Salomon and Colonel Weer made up the bulk of the

Federal force which included German immigrants, Wisconsin volunteers, Kansas troops, and the three Indian Home Guard regiments. General Salomon, in overall command, was under orders not to bring on any battles until other converging Federal columns reached the area. Yet 150 cavalry troopers and two howitzers were dispatched from the Union camp to probe the Confederate position at Newtonia. The detachment briefly skirmished with a group of Rebels on the 29th before withdrawing. On the morning of September 30, they joined another force from the Sarcoxie camp consisting of several companies of Wisconsin infantry, Kansas cavalry, Indian troops, and three cannon. Apparently unaware of the seriously large numbers of additional Confederates encamped within striking distance, the reinforced Union detachment attacked the Southerners at Newtonia, and by 7:00 A.M. the battle had grown to major proportions.

Colonel Douglas Cooper, as senior Confederate officer, took overall command of the various Southern units that rallied to the defense of Newtonia. The outnumbered Yanks had much more than they had bargained for, and when Cooper's Choctaw and Chickasaw warriors, under Lt. Col. Tandy Walker, dramatically galloped right through the town in a howling charge, the blue line broke to pieces. Pursued for approximately six miles, the surviving Yanks met General Salomon that afternoon advancing with his main force. Rallying the broken columns, Salomon renewed the battle with fresh troops, but large numbers of his men gave way toward evening, and he was forced to retreat back to Sarcoxie in the darkness. The Federals had suffered 50 killed, 80 wounded, and 115 missing that day. The victorious Confederates had only 12 killed, 63 wounded, and 3 missing.

However, the Battle of Newtonia was a hollow victory for the Southerners for by October 3, General Schofield had accumulated 18,000 troops in the Newtonia area, including General Blunt and the balance of his force, soon to be designated as the 1st Division of Schofield's "Army of the Frontier." The Yanks entered the town on October 4, and most of the white Confederate troops fled to Arkansas to rejoin General Hindman's army.

Cooper's Native American forces withdrew back to Indian Territory. The victorious Army of the Frontier crossed the border into Arkansas and camped at the Pea Ridge battlefield.

At the Pea Ridge encampment, General Schofield ordered General Blunt to march to the vicinity of Fort Wayne where reports indicated Cooper's force was encamped. It was feared that Cooper and Watie would disrupt the flow of supplies and communication between the Army of the Frontier in northwest Arkansas and its base at Fort Scott, Kansas. Thus Blunt was given the mission to soundly defeat the Confederate Native Americans along the Arkansas-Indian Territory border.

James Blunt was a tough little Kansas abolitionist who had been a medical doctor before the war. He was a strong supporter of U.S. senator James Lane, the fiery antislavery orator and Kansas Jayhawker who personally led bloody raids into Missouri to avenge similar raids into his home state of Kansas. Blunt had received his officer's commission as a result of his political affiliation with Lane, but he proved to be a real "scrapper," ready and willing to fight the enemy with bold and decisive military prowess. However, his abrasive personality coupled with his short, chubby physique had earned him the unflattering nickname of "Fat Boy" among his own troops.

General Blunt left his 1st Brigade, under General Salomon, at Pea Ridge to scout the countryside while he marched to the Indian Territory border with the 2nd and 3rd Brigades of his division. Blunt's force reached Bentonville, Arkansas, by mid-afternoon on October 21. They halted just long enough to eat supper and feed their horses before moving out again. Most of the troops had been on the march for the last 36 hours and now, according to the "Fat Boy's" plan, they were to continue their forced march overnight in order to be in position to attack Cooper's warriors at dawn. By 6:00 P.M., the exhausted Union army had moved out of Bentonville heading west into the sunset toward Fort Wayne. The cavalry units soon outdistanced the rest of the army so they halted to get some badly needed rest while the rest of the force drew together. When the lead units of

Maj. Gen. James G. Blunt

infantry began to close up, they too fell out to the side of the road waiting for the rear of the column to come up. Soon most of the Federal army was sound asleep, stretched out for miles along the side of the Maysville Road which led to Fort Wayne. General Blunt, ahead of his army accompanied by his staff, gave the order to move out. The bugler did not sound the order for fear of warning the nearby enemy, so Blunt's command was passed on by word of mouth. The nearest unit, the 2nd Kansas Cavalry whose troopers had gotten more rest than anyone else, mounted up and accompanied Blunt and his staff down the road. However, the rest of Blunt's army remained sound asleep, oblivious to their commander's orders.

Coming within sight of a large and fine home in the early morning darkness, Blunt displayed his flair for the dramatic by hastily disguising himself as a Confederate soldier who had just escaped from being held prisoner by the Union Army and was searching for his way back to Cooper's camp. Playing his role like a true Thespian, Blunt soon convinced the matron of the household, whose husband was serving with Cooper, that he was who he claimed to be. The lady informed Blunt that the main Confederate camp was indeed three miles beyond the town of Maysville at the site of old Fort Wayne, just as he suspected. After thanking the lady for her Southern hospitality, he returned to his staff down the road and proceeded toward Maysville with what he thought was his entire army. He sent two companies of cavalry around the village to intercept anyone trying to warn Cooper's camp and then rode back to the rear of his column to see if it had closed up. To his astonishment, he could find only one company of the 2nd Kansas Cavalry! He sent a messenger down the road with orders for all units to move up on the "double quick." Then at dawn on October 22, the daring Blunt proceeded to launch a surprise attack with only three companies of cavalry, hoping to hold the enemy at bay until his main force arrived on the battlefield. The surprised Confederates, unaware of how ridiculously small the attacking force was, immediately went on the defensive. Soon, additional Union cavalry detachments began to gallop onto the field, including

Blunt convinced the lady of the house that he was a Confederate soldier.

the remainder of the 2nd Kansas with their two mountain howitzers. A thunderous artillery duel between the two forces commenced immediately. At last Cooper sensed his foe's weakness in numbers and attempted to flank the Union position. But the timely arrival of Colonel Phillips' 3rd Indian Home Guard and the 6th Kansas Cavalry countered the Confederate thrust. Blunt then ordered a general advance, and Cooper's warriors fell back in disorder. Rebel artillery horses fell in thrashing heaps around their gun limbers as they came within the gunsights of Yankee cavalry carbines. Cooper soon lost all of his cannon without the horses to withdraw them from the field. The 3rd Indian Home Guard and the 6th Kansas Cavalry pursued the forces of Cooper and Watie for seven miles across the fiery autumn countryside. Confederate battle losses totaled 6 killed, 30 wounded, and 26 missing. Union casualties numbered 5 killed and 5 wounded. Blunt's victorious troops returned to the nearby village of Maysville back across the Arkansas line, showing off a trophy of their day's work—a captured Rebel battle flag.

Far to the southwest, on the night of October 23-24, 1862, there was a major assault conducted near the Confederate Indian Agency near Fort Cobb, although it was apparently not at all connected with the war. Most of the people of the Tonkawa Tribe, who were camped on Tonkawa Creek near the agency, were brutally massacred by an attacking force made up of miscellaneous other tribes. The agency itself, which supported the Tonkawas, was destroyed as well. Fortunately for the Tonkawas, a portion of their band was absent from the main camp on a hunting trip; otherwise the entire tribe would have been exterminated, which was indeed the goal of the attacking force. The attempt to annihilate the Tonkawas was due to the fact that the tribe had the reputation of actively practicing cannibalism. Neighboring tribes found this dietary habit to be not only repulsive but also threatening. The Shawnee, Delaware, Cherokee, Creek, Seminole, Wichita, Waco, Caddo, and a couple of lesser known tribes were all represented in the attacking force. The survivors of the Tonkawa Tribe fled to Fort Arbuckle for refuge and eventually went back to Texas from where they had been removed. Nearly 20 years after the Civil War, the few descendants of the Tonkawas returned to Indian Territory, settling on a small reservation in what is now Kay County.

Meanwhile, Cooper and Watie had retreated south of the Arkansas River following the Battle of Fort Wayne. A number of Cherokee families loyal to the Union then attempted to return to their homes in Indian Territory. Blunt marched his men back to northwest Arkansas, and Schofield withdrew his 2nd and 3rd Divisions from the region, leaving Blunt and the 1st Division to hold the area for the Union. Confederate General Thomas Hindman's attempt to retake northwest Arkansas met with defeat as General Blunt once again emerged victorious at the Battle of Prairie Grove on December 7, 1862.

Impressed with the performance of his Native American troops, Blunt sent them on a special mission in late December. Colonel William Phillips, now in overall command of the Indian Brigade which consisted of all three regiments, was ordered back to Indian Territory in an attempt to finish off Stand Watie and Colonel Cooper. Phillips was a capable and dedicated officer who had immigrated to the United States from Scotland. He went to Kansas in 1855 as a correspondent for the *New York Tribune* and became actively involved in abolitionist activities during the Kansas-Missouri Border War. His commitment to the Union cause, as well as to his Indian troops, was rock solid.

Phillips' column rode into the Cherokee Nation on December 22 with 1,200 mounted Native American troops, two companies of the 6th Kansas Cavalry, and a battery of four artillery pieces captured from Cooper at the Battle of Fort Wayne. Pushing southwest toward the Arkansas River, he found Fort Gibson to be nearly abandoned, but located a sizable force of Confederate Indians camped nearby on the other side of the river at Fort Davis. Fort Davis had been established by General Pike who named it in honor of the president of the Confederacy. It was located just north of present-day Muskogee, Oklahoma, and occupied a hill overlooking the valley of the Arkansas River opposite the mouth of the Grand and Verdigris rivers. A prehistoric Indian mound was situated in the center of the post, and the flagstaff of the garrison stood in the center of this mound. The Confederate colors proudly waved from that flagstaff in the crisp winter breeze as Colonel Phillips' column approached the post on December 27. His artillery unlimbered their guns and thunderously announced their belated Yuletide visit. Phillips sent forward his skirmishers, and after a brief exchange of gunfire the Confederate warriors, outnumbered and demoralized, swiftly abandoned Fort Davis to their Union foes. Phillips left the post as a pile of smoldering ruins and doggedly pursued Cooper and Watie into the Creek Nation, pillaging and burning the homes of pro-Southerners along the way.

As 1862 came to a close, the elusive Confederate warriors continued to evade their determined pursuers. Although they had been outgunned, they were not yet ready to surrender. Finally, Colonel Phillips withdrew to the Arkansas border for his winter encampment. Meanwhile in the Creek Nation, Cooper and Watie made plans to rally and resupply their dispersed commands.

CHAPTER 3

Year of Decision
1863

On January 8, 1863, Brig. Gen. William Steele, who had led a
regiment in the Confederacy's ill-fated 1862 New Mexico Campaign, took overall command of Southern forces in Indian Territory. Although Col. Douglas Cooper retained his command of
all the Confederate Indian troops, the leather-tough,
whiskey-drinking old Mexican War veteran was not pleased that
he had not been chosen by Richmond for overall command in
the Territory. This situation led to a bitter rivalry between the
two commanders which did not help the beleaguered military
position of the Confederacy in Indian Territory. Yet Steele
assumed his new command of the Territory at Fort Smith,
Arkansas, where he maintained his headquarters for more than
six months. Therefore, Cooper remained the true commander
in the field, regrouping his scattered units of Native Americans
and Texans in the southern part of Indian Territory.

With their foes far to the south, Cherokees of Union sympathy attempted to establish control in their region. The Union
Cherokee Council went into session in February at Tahlequah,
under the protection of Colonel Phillips' troops, and voted to
nullify the treaty with the Confederacy. The council also
declared its allegiance to the United States, outlawed Stand
Watie and his supporters and confiscated their property, abol-
ished slavery within the tribe, and voted for Thomas Pegg to act

Outnumbered Confederates were driven into the Grand River
and forced to swim for their lives.

as principal chief in the absence of John Ross. For the rest of the war, there would be two rival Cherokee tribal governments: one Union, one Confederate.

In the spring, General Blunt ordered Colonel Phillips to start moving Indian refugees back into the Territory once again. A large number of the displaced Native Americans had spent a rough winter in a Federal camp at Neosho, Missouri. Many, especially children, had perished during the ordeal which was made even more deadly by an outbreak of smallpox within the camp. About 1,000 Cherokee, Creek, and Seminole families began their long trek to the southwest escorted by Phillips' 3,000 troops. The Union warriors reached Park Hill outside of Tahlequah where the Cherokee families left the military column to return to what was left of their homes. Setting up camp, Phillips dispatched the reorganized 2nd Indian Home Guard and a detachment of the 6th Kansas Cavalry to scout ahead for the enemy. This force discovered that Watie had left a small Rebel garrison of Indian troops at Fort Gibson. The Union force launched a spirited charge upon the post and literally drove the outnumbered defenders into the Grand River. The Confederate survivors of the assault were forced to swim for their lives. On April 13, 1863, Colonel Phillips' main force triumphantly rode into Fort Gibson. Trailing behind the army's supply wagons were hundreds of Union Creeks and Seminoles, still homeless until their lands could also be forcibly taken from the tight grip of their Confederate foes.

Fort Gibson offered a good defensive position. Built on a bluff overlooking the Grand River, near the intersection of the Texas Road and the Arkansas River (the two main arteries of trade and travel in the Territory), the fort consisted of a couple of log block houses, two large stone buildings, and several small wood frame structures. Soon after establishing his headquarters at the fort, Phillips chose to honor his commanding officer by renaming the post Fort Blunt. Yet the new name did not prove to be popular among many of the rank-and-file soldiers, and the stronghold continued to be frequently referred to by its old name for the duration of the war. Colonel Phillips wasted no

time in strengthening the post's defenses with earthen breast-
works and immediately ordered his cavalry to comb the area
for enemy activity. Phillips realized that the stronghold was the
key to control of Indian Territory. However, one major disad-
vantage was the post's distance from its supply base: Fort Scott
was 160 miles away. For the rest of the war, half of Fort Gibson's
military activity involved protecting its line of communications
and escorting supply wagons.

Colonel Phillips subscribed to the military philosophy that
the best defense is a good offense, so he rarely missed an opportunity to strike his foes. When news arrived in his camp that a sizable force of Confederates had gathered at the community of
Webber's Falls, about 25 miles south of Fort Gibson, the colonel
personally led a 600-man detachment to give them a good lick-
ing. His mounted strike force consisted of Native American
troops drawn from all three Home Guard regiments and a battalion of the 6th Kansas Cavalry. The hard-riding Union troops
took the Confederate warriors at Webber's Falls completely by
surprise at dawn on April 25 as a session of the Confederate
Cherokee Council was preparing to meet in town. Their newly
designated principal chief, Col. Stand Watie, attempted to rally
his men, but his efforts were futile. Once again the Yanks successfully dispersed their opponents, yet once again the clash was
not a truly significant action with long-lasting results. Fourteen

Supply trains were under the constant threat of surprise attack.

Rebel warriors were killed in the gunplay that morning, while Phillips lost only one man.

After the action at Webber's Falls, two ladies came to the Federal lines from a plantation a couple of miles below the community and requested a doctor be sent to attend a wounded Confederate. Dr. Rufus Gillpatrick, a surgeon accompanying Colonel Phillips, immediately volunteered for the mission of mercy. Phillips offered him a military escort, but the doctor laughingly declined, stating that he was in no danger when going on such an errand. Nevertheless, as he approached the house where the wounded soldier lay, he was overtaken by a band of Rebels who emerged from the brush alongside the road. The ladies tried to persuade the ruffians not to shoot the good doctor, but their pleas fell on deaf ears, and Gillpatrick was brutally gunned down on the spot. The doctor was a very popular personality at Fort Gibson where all the men knew him and appreciated his good nature and generous ways. His brutal and unjust death so enraged the troops at the fort that they soon formed a vengeful detachment of horsemen who rode back to Webber's Falls and burned the town to the ground. By this time, the war in Indian Territory had become so bitter that both sides had little if any respect for their enemy. Most troops regarded their foes as no better than a pack of rabid dogs that should be exterminated.

On May 15, 1863, one of the most peculiar clashes of the war took place north of the Cherokee Nation on the Osage Reservation in Kansas. A small party of Osage warriors encountered a column of 20 blue-coated cavalry troopers crossing their land, riding northwest. Such sights were not uncommon to the tribesmen since there was a nearby U.S. Army post with which they were on friendly terms. Yet none of these soldiers looked familiar to the Indians. The troops responded nervously to the warriors' questions, and the tribesmen frowned at their vague answers. The Indians suggested they all ride together to the nearby army post. The mysterious soldiers refused and then attempted to ride away, but the Osage men tried to restrain

The doctor was brutally gunned down.

them. A shot rang out, and a tribesman flew off his pony, landing on the ground like a limp sack of grain thrown in the dust. Outnumbered, the rest of the Indians immediately galloped away, racing toward their nearby village to arouse the camp with news of the skirmish.

Led by the village's headman, Hard Rope, a war party of about 200 warriors followed the white men's trail until they finally caught sight of them in open country, about five miles from a loop in the Verdigris River near present-day Independence, Kansas. In their first charge, the Osage lost one man to the long-range marksmanship of the soldiers. Dividing his force, Hard Rope led another assault in which two troopers bit the dust. Outnumbered ten to one, the desperate bluecoats rode at breakneck speed toward a small grove of trees along the river. Dismounting, they splashed frantically through the water to a sandbar in the middle of the stream. There they made their hopeless stand against the overwhelming numbers of Osage. Expending all their ammunition, the troopers fought hand to hand with the warriors who swarmed among them like angry hornets. One by one the soldiers fell until they all lay motionless on the bloody sandbar, ready to be stripped of their equipment and uniforms. Scalps were peeled from their skulls, and their heads were severed and tossed aside as other customary mutilations were made upon their bare, twisted corpses.

Later the Osage informed the nearby army post about the battle on the Verdigris, and a detachment of the 9th Kansas Cavalry was immediately sent out to investigate. When the Kansas troopers found the gruesome scene of the massacre, they discovered various articles of Confederate origin. Later when the 9th Kansas visited Hard Rope's village, the Osage leader gave their commander some water-stained papers found in the clothing of the mysterious soldiers. The documents were official Confederate Army communiqués which explained the whole sad affair. The papers revealed that a special task force of 20 Confederate Army officers, led by Col. Charles Harrison, had been ordered by Maj. Gen. Theophilus Holmes to ride west on a diabolical mission to incite Plains Indian tribes to wage war on settlers in Kansas and Nebraska. The officers were to enlist the aid of white Confederate sympathizers out West to help them in their efforts. They had been authorized to promise arms and ammunition in return for the Indians' mercenary services. The intent of this devious plan was to draw Union Army forces from the war in Arkansas and Missouri to the far West. Interestingly, only 18 white men's bodies were found, and later it was discovered that two Southern officers had indeed survived. Colonel Warner Lewis lived to tell the tale of how he and a comrade named John Rafferty had escaped upstream under cover of the riverbank during the massacre, and after a harrowing ordeal of wilderness survival, finally made it back to friendly territory. Thus one of the most bizarre secret plots of the war came to an ill-fated end.

Meanwhile back at Fort Gibson, Colonel Phillips was growing concerned that his position was becoming precarious. Confederate Indian forces under Cooper, now a brigadier general, had regrouped and had been reinforced by new regiments of Texas cavalry and a battery of three mountain howitzers. Now outnumbering the Union troops at Fort Gibson, Cooper's army of 5,000 men had boldly marched north and set up camp only five miles south of the post on the opposite side of the Arkansas River under cover of the woods along the river valley. To make matters worse, Confederate forces just across the border in Arkansas led by Brig. Gen. William Cabell had pressured Federal troops to withdraw from their base at Fayetteville. If Cabell was to join forces with Cooper, Phillips and his men would certainly not be able to hold their fort for long. Thus urgent requests for numerous reinforcements were sent from Fort Gibson to General Blunt.

Colonel Phillips strengthened his picket posts along the Arkansas River and frequently sent out strong reconnaissance patrols to hold General Cooper south of the wide river. The Union pickets (perimeter guards) kept up a lively fire with the Confederate pickets for several weeks, yet casualties were light.

Eventually they became less hostile toward one another and even reached a point where some occasionally met on sandbars in the middle of the river to trade items.

Throughout the standoff, both sides surveyed each other's activities. General Cooper became aware of the Union force's habit of grazing their off-duty cavalry horses from morning until night within a two- or three-mile radius of the fort. With his army's renewed strength, Cooper felt confident enough to order out a detachment of troopers to turn the Yankee horses into Rebel horses. On the night of May 19, five Confederate regiments crossed the river, and about 9:00 A.M. the next morning, the Southerners burst out of the brush near the Union horse herd. Advancing rapidly, they easily overran the enemy pickets and herders and rounded up the horses. Throwing up a skirmish line, they advanced within only two miles of Fort Gibson. Fortunately for the Union force, a couple of the herders were able to reach the safety of the fort's defenses and warned the garrison of the attack. Bugles sounded the alarm, and Colonel Phillips' men sprang into action, grabbing their weapons and falling into formation. Union cavalry galloped out to engage the enemy, skirmishing briefly before falling back to the shelter of the post's earthen walls. Soon 2,000 Union troops manned their entrenchments as Colonel Phillips advanced with two battalions of dismounted Native American soldiers and a section of the 3rd Kansas Light Artillery. He clashed with the Confederates only a mile from the fort. With the help of his reinforced cavalry, Phillips drove back Cooper's advancing troops, but he was unable to retake all of his captured horse herd. Union casualties totaled 20 killed and 20 wounded; Confederate losses were uncertain, but most likely their loss was similar. If General Cooper had advanced with his entire force that day, he might have recaptured Fort Gibson for the Confederacy.

In response to Colonel Phillips' desperate requests for reinforcements, and to meet his dire need for more supplies as well, General Blunt sent a strong force of troops south, escorting a large wagon train laden with foodstuffs, ammunition, and

Yankee horses were turned into Rebel horses by Cooper's advancing troops.

equipment. The relief force consisted of six companies of the 2nd Colorado Regiment, one company of the 3rd Wisconsin Cavalry, one company each of the 9th and 14th Kansas Cavalry, and one section of the 2nd Kansas Artillery, all under the command of Lt. Col. Theodore Dodd of the 2nd Colorado. When the wagon train and its escort arrived at the army post at Baxter Springs, Kansas (about 80 miles north of Fort Gibson), additional troops were added to the column. A newly formed regiment of African-American troops, the 1st Kansas Colored Infantry under the command of Col. James M. Williams, fell in with the rest of the Union units. In addition, a detachment from Fort Gibson itself arrived at Baxter Springs to assist the train escort. Colonel Phillips had ordered out several hundred troops from the fort to intercept the column and help escort the wagon train to the safety of his stronghold. This force consisted of elements from the three Indian regiments and the 6th Kansas Cavalry, all under the command of Maj. John Foreman of the 3rd Indian Home Guard.

The long column of troops and 300 wagons lumbered along the "Military Road" which connected Fort Scott to Fort Gibson. The well-traveled road had been the scene of many a skirmish as Confederate partisans attacked supply trains on a regular basis. Even this huge train with its powerful escort would also be the target of Rebel guns before its long journey was over.

Confederate scouts kept Col. Stand Watie informed of the Union column's progress as it moved deeper into Indian Territory. With his renewed military strength, Watie planned a major attack on the Union column at the ford of Cabin Creek. On June 26, as the wagon train crossed Grand River, Union Cherokees scouting miles ahead of the column discovered their numerous horse tracks. Cautiously following the tracks, they found their source: a large force of Confederate Indians and Texans at the ford of Cabin Creek. After a sharp skirmish with some enemy pickets, the Cherokee scouts raced back to the wagons with a couple of prisoners they had managed to capture.

Upon questioning, the captive soldiers revealed that Stand Watie had more than 2,000 men anxiously waiting to attack the wagon train upon its arrival at Cabin Creek. They also confessed that General Cabell was in the vicinity as well, but he was cut off from joining forces with Colonel Watie due to high water. On the first day of July, the Union column finally arrived in the vicinity of Cabin Creek. The march had been slow since heavy rains had turned the Military Road into a muddy quagmire. However, the sluggish pace had given the three senior Union officers, Williams, Dodd, and Foreman, plenty of time to plan their strategy and tactics for the impending battle at the creek crossing.

The supply wagons were corralled on a prairie two miles from the crossing with the 6th Kansas left to guard them. The rest of the Union force moved into battle formation within sight of the Confederates who were concealed in the brush on the opposite side of the creek where they had dug rifle pits. It was already hot and humid on that morning of July 2, 1863, as U.S. Army officers bellowed out commands to their troops who nervously marched into position under sporadic gunfire from snipers across the stream. At that same moment, hundreds of miles to the east, Union and Confederate armies faced each other in a larger, more famous battle at a little town called Gettysburg. Meanwhile, on the Mississippi River, the monumental siege of Vicksburg was nearing its dramatic conclusion. The summer

of 1863 was destined to be the major turning point of the war.

The men of the 2nd Kansas Artillery unlimbered their guns and opened fire on the brush lining the south bank of Cabin Creek, hoping to soften up the Confederate positions before an all-out assault. For more than half an hour, artillery shells churned the ground and splintered trees, sending their limbs crashing down over the heads of Southern soldiers who desperately hugged the dirt in their rifle pits. Then Major Foreman, on horseback, waved his saber aloft and shouted to a company of mounted Indian troopers to follow him. In a whirlwind of fury they splashed into the rain-swollen creek. With the

The former slaves proved themselves to be true soldiers.

water up to their horses' bellies, they struggled toward the opposite bank, shouting defiantly at their enemies who rose from their rifle pits and blasted away at the charging, blue-clad warriors. Crimson puddles mingled with the muddy water as men and horses thrashed about in the stream, attempting to make their way back to the Union line. Major Foreman was among the seriously wounded. The Federal infantry had moved into position to deliver covering fire as the 9th Kansas Cavalry galloped forward to attempt a charge. Clouds of gunsmoke rolled over the water as the stubborn Kansans gained a foothold on the muddy creek bank in front of the Confederate rifles. Then Colonel Williams led his 1st Kansas Colored Infantry forward into the stream. Holding their rifles and cartridge boxes above their heads to keep their powder dry, the dauntless African-Americans sloshed through the waist-deep water to the opposite shore and formed a line of battle as bullets and buckshot flew around them. With warm adrenaline flowing through their veins, the former slaves followed their Anglo-Saxon colonel into the brush, overrunning the enemy rifle pits in a mad, fearless dash through the timber. Watie's men attempted to regroup about a quarter of a mile away on the edge of a prairie, but again they broke and ran as the Yanks surged forward. Many of the Confederates retreated to Grand River and drowned along with their horses as they tried to swim across the rain-swollen torrent of swift, deep water. Their bodies were seen hours later floating by Fort Gibson. Exact Southern losses at the Battle of Cabin Creek are unknown, but Union estimates of their enemies' casualties claim about 50 were killed and 50 wounded. Federal losses included only 3 dead and 30 wounded. The badly needed supply wagons and reinforcements finally reached Fort Gibson on July 5, much to the relief of Colonel Phillips and his hungry troops. The broader significance of the Battle of Cabin Creek was that it was one of the first actions of the war in which African-Americans fought alongside white troops—proving that it was not only possible, but even a winning combination.

Upon receiving word of the serious action at Cabin Creek and the large build-up of enemy forces in the vicinity of Fort Gibson, Gen. James Blunt took to the field himself, leading additional reinforcements from Fort Scott to Fort Gibson (or Fort Blunt, as he preferred to call it). The general and his column arrived at the post on July 11 after a forced march. Assuming command of the entire force at the fort, which now numbered about 3,000 troops with 12 artillery pieces, he immediately started planning his strategy against his foes.

Word soon arrived at Fort Gibson that General Cabell in Arkansas was planning to join forces with the Confederate army in Indian Territory. General Cooper's force of 6,000 troops, with four artillery pieces, was encamped at Honey Springs only 25 miles south of Fort Gibson. Cabell was marching from Fort Smith with 3,000 men and additional artillery to join him there for an all-out effort to retake Fort Gibson and drive the Union Army from the Territory.

The Confederate camp and supply depot at Honey Springs consisted of a frame commissary building, a log hospital, several brush arbors, and hundreds of tents. Several springs provided the camp with plenty of fresh water. By July of 1863, the Honey Springs camp was the most important Confederate installation in Indian Territory. It also was the primary objective of General Blunt who planned to strike Cooper before he could be reinforced by Cabell. At midnight on July 15, General Blunt rode out of Fort Gibson. At last the time had come for a decisive, major battle in Indian Territory—a clash of arms that would determine the outcome of the war and the fate of the people in the region. The day of reckoning was at hand.

Most of Blunt's force crossed the rain-swollen Arkansas River on rafts. Unfortunately, several Indian troops drowned when they tried to swim across the river. By 10:00 P.M. on July 16, the Union army was on the south bank of the Arkansas and began marching toward Elk Creek and Honey Springs. About midnight a skirmish occurred near Chimney Mountain as the Union vanguard collided with a Confederate scouting party.

The clash took place during a rain shower, and it was then that the Southern soldiers first noticed a serious problem which would plague their army during the upcoming battle: some of the gunpowder had absorbed moisture from the wet weather and would not fire. Unfortunately for the Confederates, their powder supply was made up of cheap, low-grade Mexican gunpowder which had been rendered even more unreliable than usual by the recent intermittent rains. This compounded another serious problem for the Southern soldiers—they were severely outgunned by Blunt's force. Although they outnumbered the approaching Union army by two to one, about one-quarter of the Confederate Indian troops were without adequate firearms. Blunt's infantry carried standard long-range Springfield rifles, and his cavalry had up-to-date breech-loading carbines as well as revolvers. In comparison, Cooper's troops had a wide variety of weapons, many of which were captured Federal guns and civilian firearms, including shotguns which were effective only at a very close range. Also Cooper had only four light artillery pieces: three mountain howitzers and a unique, even smaller field piece known as a "mountain rifle." Only eighteen of these small, experimental cannon were manufactured in Richmond during the war, and somehow, one piece made it out to the Indian frontier. The mountain rifle had a bronze barrel which was rifled to take a 2¼-inch-diameter explosive shell. Meanwhile, Blunt's army had twelve artillery pieces: six big "Napoleon" cannon designed to fire 12-pound projectiles; two equally large, model 1841 field guns which fired 6-pound projectiles; and four mountain howitzers like Cooper's.

At daylight on July 17, the first clash of battle took place as the 6th Kansas Cavalry charged a force of about 500 Confederate cavalrymen drawn up in combat formation on the Texas Road. The stubborn veterans of the 6th Kansas drove the Rebel troopers south in a flurry of revolver fire. At 8:00 A.M., the Federal army encountered General Cooper's entire force ready for action in a defensive line on the north side of Elk Creek. Mercifully, Blunt halted his exhausted troops for a brief rest and a quick meal from their haversacks. The men had been on the march all night long and took a much-needed break as their commander rode forward with his staff to better view the enemy position. The Union command group soon began drawing fire from sharpshooters and was forced to seek cover after one staff member was shot dead from his saddle.

Another cloudburst cooled the sweaty troops, and they filled their canteens from muddy puddles in the trail. About 9:30 A.M., General Blunt formed his men in two columns on both sides of the Texas Road. Colonel William R. Judson of the 6th Kansas was put in charge of the cavalry brigade on the west side, which included the 2nd Colorado, the 1st Indian Home Guard, and the 6th Kansas. On the east side, Col. William Phillips led his 2nd Indian Home Guard, the 3rd Wisconsin, and Col. James Williams' 1st Kansas Colored Infantry. With drums rolling and flags unfurled for battle, the Union force marched south toward Elk Creek where their foes nervously awaited the bloody onslaught. When Blunt's troops were within a quarter of a mile from the Confederate army, they were given the command to form into "line of battle." Facing them in the timber lining the creek, with their rifles and shotguns, bayonets and Bowie knives, were General Cooper's ragged but determined troops. Cooper faced the Yanks with two Cherokee regiments (minus Stand Watie who had been sent on a diversionary cavalry movement to Webber's Falls), two Creek regiments under Col. Daniel McIntosh, the 20th and 29th Texas Cavalry Regiments, the 5th Texas Partisan Rangers, the 1st Choctaw and Chickasaw Mounted Rifles led by Col. Tandy Walker, and the four-gun battery of light artillery under Capt. R. W. Lee.

The decisive battle that was to be known as the "Gettysburg of Indian Territory" opened at approximately 10:00 A.M. with an artillery duel that lasted more than an hour. Captain Lee's small battery fired the opening round and, much to his credit, Lee gave the Union guns a tough contest, even scoring a direct hit on one of the big Federal cannons. An artillery sergeant, a private, and four horses were killed in the resulting explosion that destroyed one of Blunt's Napoleon guns. However, captains Edward Smith and Henry Hopkins, commanding the Federal artillery, were not to be outdone. Concentrated fire from the Union guns soon wrecked one of the Confederate howitzers, killing its entire crew and horse team in the thunderous shelling. Meanwhile, the crew of the Rebel mountain rifle utilized the accuracy of their little cannon to attempt to land a few shells in the midst of a group of Union officers who could be seen on high ground beyond the enemy battle line. They killed one of General Blunt's aides and narrowly missed Captain Smith as he directed the fire of his artillery.

Union infantry and dismounted cavalry soon moved forward and opened fire on the Confederate battle line in the brush along Elk Creek. For more than two hours both sides blasted away at each other in a conflagration of smoke and flame. Utilizing their superior numbers, the Southerners attempted to flank the Union position on the left. Companies C, F, and H of the 6th Kansas met the Rebel threat on the flank and, with the help of their Sharps carbines, hurled the Southerners back.

Becoming overenthusiastic, the 2nd Indian Home Guard advanced far out in front of the Union line and exposed itself to "friendly fire." The Federal army ceased fire while the Native American troops fell back into their proper position. Texas troops took note of the lull in enemy gunfire and observed the Union warriors withdrawing from their front. Believing the Federal army was about to break, the dismounted 29th Texas Cavalry advanced to within 25 paces of the 1st Kansas Colored Infantry whose presence was hidden by the thick clouds of gunsmoke that hung in the tall prairie grass. The African-American troops, whose badly wounded regimental commander had already been carried from the field, leveled a point-blank volley of devastating rifle fire into the onrushing Texans. Their first line was completely destroyed. Then a second volley tore into their ranks, causing the survivors to turn and flee in total disorder. As the Texans retreated, the entire Confederate defense line suddenly collapsed like a row of falling dominoes. General Cooper realized it was hopeless to try to hold his line at this point and ordered his artillery to withdraw immediately across

The 29th Texas reeled under a hail of devastating gunfire.

the bridge over Elk Creek. Many a Texas trooper fell while defending the bridge long enough for the Confederate artillery to rumble across its thick wooden planks to the other side. Cooper succeeded in directing an orderly retreat for a mile and half down the Texas Road to the Honey Springs camp and supply depot. There Colonel Walker's Choctaw and Chickasaw troopers and two squadrons of Texas cavalry formed a new defensive line, delaying the Federal advance long enough to save the main portion of the Confederate army, including the artillery and supply wagons. All the buildings and supplies at Honey Springs were set afire by the retreating Confederates, but Blunt's victorious soldiers arrived soon enough to save large quantities of bacon, flour, sorghum, and salt.

By 2:00 P.M. the battle had fizzled out. Cooper's broken, demoralized army moved east as a steady rain began to fall. Only two hours later, his force linked up with General Cabell's 3,000 troops who were too late to save the Southern Cause in Indian Territory. The combined Confederate forces soon retreated south to the Canadian River. Despite the heavy gunfire and frantic troop maneuvers, the battle casualties had been light. General Cooper reported his losses as 134 killed and wounded and 47 taken prisoner. General Blunt listed his casualties as only 17 killed and 60 wounded.

The Battle of Honey Springs, also known as the Battle of Elk Creek, near present-day Rentiesville, Oklahoma, marked the climax of large-scale massed Confederate military resistance to the Federal government in Indian Territory. Never again would the Confederates be able to assemble a full-sized army to combat their foes in the region. Although the conflict in Indian Territory would continue for two more agonizing years, the South had in fact already lost the war when the last Confederate soldier fell at the bridge over Elk Creek on that rainy day in July of 1863.

Following the Federal victory at Honey Springs, General Blunt marched his army back to Fort Gibson to be resupplied in preparation for further offensive operations. More cavalry reinforcements arrived at the fort from Kansas, boosting the strength of Blunt's force to more than 4,500 troops. The general had received news of Cabell's force linking up with Cooper's, and he was determined to maintain the offensive against the Confederate army until it was destroyed. Meanwhile in the Southern camp, Gen. William Steele had arrived to take personal command of the demoralized army, much to the displeasure of General Cooper.

On the evening of August 22, General Blunt led his army out of Fort Gibson, marching south toward the Confederate camp on the Canadian River. After covering about 60 miles in only 48 hours, the Union army arrived at its objective only to find that the camp ground had been abandoned. In one of the most important and fateful decisions of the war in Indian Territory, the Confederate commanders had chosen to split forces and retreat. Cabell marched back toward Arkansas, Steele and Cooper withdrew farther south toward the town of Perryville, and McIntosh took his Creek warriors west toward the headwaters of the Canadian. Thus ended all possibility of another truly decisive, strategically important battle being fought in the Territory. Instead, the tedious, deadly game of cat and mouse would resume between the well-equipped Federal troops and the ragged Confederate warriors. All the victories and defeats that were to follow in the region would be short-lived and fleeting, like the gunsmoke that drifted across their half-forgotten battlefields, disappearing in a hazy fog.

However, the "Fat Boy" had marched south for two days in order to fight, and he was determined to do so, one way or the other. On the morning of August 26, Blunt learned from his scouts that Steele, Cooper, and Watie were only 25 miles to the south, and he promptly moved out in pursuit. Soon, the vanguard of the Union army came in contact with the Confederate rear guard. Blunt ordered his Indian troops forward to form a long skirmish line. The Union warriors moved through the brush, and whenever contact was made with the enemy, a strong force of Federal cavalry was ordered forward to push the Rebels back. In this manner, Blunt stayed on the trail of his foes throughout the day. At 8:00 P.M. the spunky general and his confident troops reached the vicinity of Perryville. The desperate

Confederate commanders had decided to make a stand and had placed two howitzers on the road leading into town with their troops posted behind makeshift barricades of wagons, boxes, and barrels. The action began about dusk when the 6th Kansas Cavalry dismounted and deployed on each side of the road. The troopers then advanced, rapidly firing their deadly Sharps carbines at the nervous, outnumbered Confederates who responded with an assortment of various muzzle-loading firearms from behind their pitiful defenses. Then the Federal artillery opened up, and the Rebel warriors skedaddled into the darkness, heading toward the Red River. Perryville was a Confederate supply base, so Blunt's men loaded up all they could carry and set the rest afire.

Following the action at Perryville, General Blunt devised a bold plan to divide his force, sending half in pursuit of McIntosh's Creek warriors while the other half marched east to take Fort Smith, Arkansas. In the early morning darkness on August 27, Colonel Judson led his brigade, including the 1st Indian Regiment, 2nd Colorado, and 6th Kansas Cavalry, deeper west in the Territory, while General Blunt rode off to Arkansas with the rest of his army. During Judson's hard-riding pursuit of the Confederate warriors, McIntosh's force steadily dissolved, losing men to desertion every step of the way. Soon there were only about 150 Native American troops left in McIntosh's command. Judson's brigade had destroyed the Creek force without having to fire a shot since they left Perryville. The saddle-sore U.S. troopers returned to Fort Gibson without losing a single man during the expedition. Soon, starving, ragged deserters from McIntosh's command arrived at Fort Gibson nearly every day, declaring their loyalty to the Union and begging for food.

By this time, the Confederate forces in Indian Territory were so demoralized and destitute of supplies that, for the most part, they were ineffective as combat troops. Only one unit kept the Southern Cause alive in the region with daring raids on Federal camps, patrols, and supply wagons—Col. Stand Watie's Cherokee Mounted Rifles. Watie had become a master of guerrilla

Renowned Confederate Cherokee leader, Gen. Stand Watie

warfare, utilizing hit-and-run tactics in countless strikes against his Federal foes; keeping his men supplied with captured Union gear, weapons, ammunition, and raw foodstuffs. His charismatic leadership and little victories in numerous skirmishes kept the spark of rebellion alive in the hearts of many Confederate sympathizers in Indian Territory for the difficult remaining days of 1863. To most Native Americans, and even to many whites in the region, Stand Watie had come to symbolize the fury and defiance of the Southern Cause.

Unfortunately for the Confederates, such leadership as Watie's was not common among other commanders in Indian Territory. Many of the Southern units, including all Native American forces, were allowed to choose their own officers by a vote. The winners of such popularity contests were frequently not disciplinarian combat leaders. As a matter of fact, General Cooper complained of how his Indian troops often visited their homes whenever they wished, being absent for long periods of time. In contrast, Union Indian regiments were officered principally by white leaders appointed by the military, and they were not usually very concerned with pleasing their troops, although they made sure their men were properly fed and equipped so as to be in good fighting condition.

The days of '63 turned slowly, like a millstone grinding grains of misery as the merciless guerrilla war raged on in Indian Territory. As Watie's raids grew more frequent, Union soldiers became less patient with the civilians in the region who supported him. U.S. cavalry patrols left destruction in their wake, as burnt homes and murdered citizens became commonplace in the Territory. Livestock became very scarce. Cavalry units on both sides "requisitioned" nearly every horse they saw, and all pigs, chickens, and cattle soon became army chow. As a matter of fact, a dubious money-making scheme involving cattle sales to the U.S. government (for use by the army) was investigated in the autumn of 1863. An honest army officer in Kansas, Maj. Preston Plumb, discovered that a group of cattle dealers were paying Osage tribesmen to steal livestock down in Indian Territory and bring them back to Kansas for two dollars a head. The dealers would then sell the cattle to the government for very inflated prices. Major Plumb promptly busted up the cattle rustling operation. Evidence indicated that a number of prominent citizens and even several U.S. Army officers were involved in the scam, but charges were discreetly dropped.

Most farms in Indian Territory also had their crops quickly consumed or destroyed by soldiers. With no livestock and no crops, many families suddenly found themselves literally without food. Nearly 18,000 pro-Southern Cherokees and Creeks fled south to the Choctaw and Chickasaw lands to seek food and shelter and to escape the wrath of the Federal government. In an ironic reversal of the tragic 1861 Union Indian refugee problem in Kansas, the Confederate government suddenly found itself burdened with thousands of hungry, homeless Native Americans encamped at Confederate posts near the Red River.

As the miserable refugees attempted to prepare for the coming winter, Steele and Cooper, still reluctant allies, consulted their maps and supply lists as they vainly attempted to devise a plan to retake Fort Gibson. Despite the arrival of 1,000 additional Texan troops under Col. Richard M. Gano, Steele was still not confident enough to launch an offensive. Instead, he urged Col. Stand Watie to saddle up for another series of raids. In November, Watie outflanked the Union lines around Fort Gibson and attacked Union Cherokees at Tahlequah, burning the tribe's capital city as well as Chief John Ross' mansion at nearby Park Hill. The following month he rode beyond Indian Territory, skirmishing with his blue-coated foes in southwest Missouri.

As 1863 finally drew to a close, General Steele, frustrated by what he viewed as a no-win situation and mentally exhausted by the constant feuding and criticism of Cooper, as well as Watie, requested to be relieved of his command in Indian Territory. On December 11, he received the official order granting his request. The same order assigned a new commander to replace Steele, and once again Richmond overlooked Douglas Cooper, bringing in another outsider to take charge. For Cooper and many others, the war had become insufferably tedious.

Col. William A. Phillips

CHAPTER 4

A Blazing Finale
1864-65

The new commander of all Confederate forces in Indian Territory, Gen. Samuel B. Maxey, was a veteran of the Army of Tennessee. Maxey, a good soldier dedicated to the Southern Cause, planned to conduct a more aggressive campaign than his predecessor. However, while Maxey was still drilling and supplying his men in preparation for action, Col. William Phillips set forth from Fort Gibson, on February 1, with about 1,500 cavalry troopers on a "scorched earth" march south to demonstrate the power and wrath of the Federal government and the futility of opposing it. Phillips' force was made up of elements of the 1st and 3rd Indian Home Guard regiments and a portion of the 14th Kansas Cavalry.

Two months earlier, President Abraham Lincoln had a proclamation written in each Indian language in which he offered pardons to any Native Americans willing to cease hostilities against the Federal government and support the Union. Phillips decided to deliver copies of this proclamation to tribal leaders along with a letter of his own which stated in part, "The great Government of the United States will soon crush all enemies. Let me know if you want to be among them." Before starting out on his punitive mission, the Scottish colonel set the tone for his expedition by telling his men, "Those who are still in arms are rebels, and ought to die. Do not kill a prisoner after he has surrendered. But I do not ask you to take prisoners. I do ask you to make your footsteps severe and terrible." Phillips' men laid waste the countryside, destroying farms and wiping out what little livestock remained. Phillips rode almost as far as the Texas border, burning homes and barns and gunning down anyone who opposed him. His grim Union horde burned a path to the Middle Boggy River within 20 miles of Fort Washita. The Southerners had a supply base located along the river known as Boggy Depot near present-day Atoka, Oklahoma. Colonel Phillips dispatched a detachment of 350 men and one section of howitzers, all under the command of Maj. Charles Willets, to seize the outpost.

The Confederate force at Boggy Depot numbered less than 90 men, and they had no artillery. On February 9, Major Willets led a surprise attack on the Confederate camp, initiating a savage struggle which lasted about half an hour. The surviving defenders made their way south to the camp of Lt. Col. John Jumper's Seminole troops. Jumper ordered his men to saddle up at once, and they rode immediately to Boggy Depot to launch a counterattack. Upon arriving at the scene of the action, Jumper and his men found that the enemy troopers had already left, returning to Phillips' main camp. The Yanks had left a grisly scene of carnage and destruction. Willets' men, following their commander's orders, had taken no prisoners. Wounded Confederates, left behind when their comrades retreated, had been butchered like hogs with their throats cut from ear to ear. The defenders' casualties numbered 49 dead.

Colonel Phillips' infamous march lasted nearly a month. He covered about 400 miles, reported he killed 250 Confederates, and returned to Fort Blunt (Fort Gibson) without losing a single man. Yet his mission had failed to break the spirit of Confederate defiance of Federal authority in Indian Territory. As a matter of fact, the death and destruction he left in the wake of his march only served to strengthen the resolve of Southern sympathizers to fight back for another year.

As if the Confederates in Indian Territory didn't have enough

problems, discord and contention between their top commanders continued. General Douglas Cooper still felt that he should
hold the top military position in the Territory and expressed his
opinion on the matter in a letter to none other than President
Jefferson Davis himself. Cooper personally knew the Confederate president, having served well as a captain in Davis' illustrious
regiment of Mississippi Volunteers during the Mexican War
nearly 20 years earlier. Cooper's letter set some political wheels
in motion which would later result in Maxey being reassigned to
a different command.

In the meantime, the Confederate forces underwent a
change in unit and command structure on the brigade level as
Maxey attempted to reorganize his army. The troops of the
Creek and Seminole Nations were brigaded with Watie's troops
of the Cherokee Nation. This force was designated as the 1st
Indian Cavalry Brigade and consisted of the following units: 1st
Cherokee Regiment under Col. Robert C. Parks, 2nd Cherokee Regiment under Col. William Penn Adair (who had been a
private in the ranks until his election to colonel), the Cherokee Battalion under Maj. Joseph A. Scales, 1st Creek Regiment
under Col. Daniel N. McIntosh, 2nd Creek Regiment under Col.
Chilly McIntosh, the Creek Squadron under Capt. R. Kenard,
the Osage Battalion under Maj. Broke Arm (these warriors were
the minority of the Osage Tribe who cast their lot with the Confederacy), and the Seminole Battalion under Lt. Col. John
Jumper. The commander of the 1st Indian Cavalry Brigade was
Col. Stand Watie.

The 2nd Indian Cavalry Brigade, which composed the
remainder of all Confederate Native American military units,
consisted of the following: 1st Chickasaw Battalion under Lt.
Col. Lemuel M. Reynolds, 1st Choctaw Battalion under Lt. Col.
Jackson McCurtain, 1st Choctaw and Chickasaw Regiment under
Lt. Col. James Riley, 2nd Choctaw Regiment under Col. Simpson
Folsom, and the Reserve Squadron (consisting of warriors of the
Caddo Tribe) under Capt. George Washington, who was a
Caddo chief. The commander of the 2nd Indian Cavalry Brigade

was the Confederate hero of the Battle of Newtonia, Missouri, Col. Tandy Walker. Walker was of mixed Choctaw and white blood. He had been the Choctaws' first principal chief after the Tribe's settlement west of the Mississippi in Indian Territory.

Colonel Walker's first major duty after being designated commander of the 2nd Indian Cavalry Brigade was to accompany Gen. Samuel Maxey and Col. Richard Gano's Texas Brigade to Arkansas in order to assist Gen. Sterling Price's army in holding back a Federal army under Gen. Frederick Steele advancing from Union-held Little Rock. Thus Colonel Walker found himself engaged in one of the most infamous battles of the entire war at Poison Springs, Arkansas, on April 18, 1864. At Poison Springs the Confederates surprised a U.S. supply train of nearly 200 wagons loaded with forage and completely overran the outnumbered Union force guarding it all. The wagon train's escort included the troops of the 1st Kansas Colored Infantry, heroes of the battles at Cabin Creek and Honey Springs. Texas troops at Poison Springs saw their chance for vengeance. The merciless Texans, many of whom had suffered defeat by the African-Americans at the battles back in Indian Territory, gunned down any black soldiers who attempted to surrender. The 1st Kansas was decimated in one of the largest massacres of African-Americans in the war, second only to the attack on Fort Pillow, Tennessee. As for the role played by Colonel Walker and his 2nd Indian Cavalry during the battle, they fought well, capturing a battery of Union artillery.

African-American soldiers in the war west of the Mississippi were well aware of their extraordinary position of danger on the battlefield. They knew if they were overcome by their Confederate foes, they would most likely be killed rather than taken prisoner. And if they were "lucky" enough to be taken prisoner rather than slaughtered, then they would be returned to slavery. Back in June of 1863, the commander of the Confederate Trans-Mississippi Department, Gen. Edmund Kirby Smith, issued an official order that all black troops and their white officers be given no quarter in battle (killed rather than taken prisoner).

Although there seemed to be a similar, unofficial rule in the war east of the Mississippi, out West it was an unquestioned, documented, military order. This situation would explain, in part, why African-Americans were such fierce fighters in battles such as Cabin Creek and Honey Springs.

The psychology behind the Confederate soldiers' total lack of mercy for black prisoners can be explained in a number of ways. Perhaps the Southerners sought vengeance on former servants who dared to rise up against their "masters" in what they perceived as a bloody slave revolt which had cost the lives of thousands. Most Southerners were deeply, even fanatically, religious, and some could reference biblical passages which they believed condoned slavery, such as Titus, Chapter 2, verses 9-10: "Exhort servants to be obedient unto their own masters, and to please them well in all things; not answering again; not purloining, but shewing all good fidelity; that they may adorn the doctrine of God our Saviour in all things." Ironically, most Confederate soldiers never owned a single slave; they could not afford one.

After the atrocity at Poison Springs, the survivors of the 1st Kansas and their comrades in the 2nd Kansas Colored Infantry, as well as all their white officers, decided they too would not take prisoners. This situation of course gave an especially vicious and desperate nature to all clashes between Confederates and African-Americans in the region. "Remember Poison Springs!" became the battle cry of black troops west of the Mississippi River.

After his return from Poison Springs and the campaign in Arkansas, General Maxey stepped up Confederate military activity in Indian Territory, sending out frequent cavalry patrols. The renewed aggressiveness of the Confederates south of the Arkansas River had the effect of discouraging all attempts at farming by the Union refugees who had returned to their homes from Kansas. Thus a new influx of dependent Indian families arrived at Fort Gibson seeking food and protection. This swelled the number of Native American refugees encamped around the fort to 16,000. All cried out for government food, clothing, and shelter.

In the midst of this tense atmosphere of renewed military threats, shocking news arrived at Fort Gibson that a steamboat carrying supplies to the post from Fort Smith had been attacked and captured on the Arkansas River. Colonel Stand Watie had struck again, and this time he had captured the Union steamer *J.R. Williams* carrying the largest military supply cargo ever sent by water into Indian Territory. On June 15, Watie had laid in wait for the vessel at a carefully chosen spot called Pleasant Bluff, overlooking the river, with three artillery pieces and a detachment of Indian cavalry concealed from view in the brush. As the picturesque sternwheeler came within range, the Confederate guns opened up on the ship with thunderous accuracy, hitting the smokestack, pilot house, and then the boiler which spewed steam over the decks. The steamer's military guard, Lt. Horace Cook and 25 men of the 12th Kansas Infantry, returned fire with their rifles as the ship ran aground on the north bank of the river opposite Watie's force. With the river as a defensive barrier, Lieutenant Cook hoped to defend the *J.R. Williams* until reinforcements arrived. However, much to Cook's dismay, he soon observed the ship's captain and another officer traveling to the south shore in a large yawl. Suddenly, his foes had a convenient means of reaching the opposite shore in preparation for an assault. Therefore, Cook and his men beat a hasty retreat, most heading toward Fort Smith, while a few reached a nearby Union camp and alerted the troops of the river ambush.

Watie's men secured the vessel and attached ropes to it, managing to maneuver the craft to a sandbar near the south side of the river where it could be unloaded. Like a victorious band of pirates, they jubilantly pillaged the steamer, and soon many rode off with as much booty as their horses could carry. Later in the day, a 200-man detachment of the Union 2nd Indian Home Guard under Col. John Ritchie (he had been given his old command back) arrived at the scene, having ridden from their camp only 10 miles distant. Ritchie's men opened fire on Watie and his few remaining troops. Before withdrawing, Watie set the steamboat afire to prevent it from falling back into Federal hands and the wooden vessel was quickly engulfed by flames. Its blazing structure soon collapsed upon itself and slipped beneath the river, leaving only a few skeletal remains sticking above the water as a reminder of war's cruelty.

Although nothing strategically significant was gained by Watie's steamboat adventure, his sensational exploit electrified Southern sympathizers in the region, boosting their morale and inspiring them to carry on the war effort. Soon after his victory at Pleasant Bluff, near present-day Tamaha, Oklahoma, Stand Watie received orders notifying him of his promotion to the rank of brigadier general, dated retroactive to May 10, 1864. Watie had become the only Native American in the war to attain a general's rank.

Meanwhile, the other two Confederate generals in Indian Territory, Maxey and Cooper, seemed to spend more time fighting each other than battling Yanks. Finally on July 21, a directive was received from the Confederate secretary of war designating the Indian Territory as a separate military district with Gen. Douglas Cooper in overall command. General Maxey was assigned to a new command in Texas. Cooper's letter to his Mexican War comrade had finally produced results. The hard-drinking old Indian agent must have paused to reflect upon his long-awaited promotion. At last he was in total command of the most impoverished, undisciplined, and demoralized military domain in the entire Confederacy. What kind of honor was this that had been bestowed upon him? To be handed a broken, rusty sword with which to fight a hopeless battle against overwhelming odds—was this his quest? Now the time had come to clean and sharpen that poor, busted blade and ride forth to meet his fate.

General Cooper immediately saddled up for a bold march into Arkansas, briefly diverting Union military attention in the region to Fort Smith. On July 27, a detachment of Cooper's force, consisting of Choctaws and Texans led by Col. Richard Gano, sprang a devastating surprise attack on a Union cavalry outpost just south of Fort Smith at Massard Prairie. The camp

The pillaged riverboat was set afire.

was manned by several companies of the 6th Kansas Cavalry. Their commander, Maj. David Mefford, rallied his men as the first shots rang out and directed a desperate fighting retreat toward the Union fortifications of Fort Smith. Yet it was a futile effort. The cavalry's horses had been stampeded, and the dismounted troopers were soon surrounded by overwhelming numbers of hard-riding Rebel warriors. Finally, 127 Yanks were captured after 11 had been killed and 20 wounded. Gano's losses included 9 dead and 26 wounded.

On July 30, General Cooper advanced on the strong Federal force at Fort Smith with his motley, small-scale army. General Stand Watie, who had been given overall command of both Indian cavalry brigades upon the recent promotion of Cooper, helped drive back Union troops before the fort's defenses. This amazing display of Confederate bravery and determination was followed by an artillery duel until nightfall when Cooper finally withdrew back toward Indian Territory. His failed assault on Fort Smith was the last major foray of the war by Confederate Indian forces outside of their Territory.

General Cooper was not yet ready to lay down his sword, and once again the Confederates relied on guerrilla warfare to carry on their fight in Indian Territory. Small but deadly Rebel cavalry raids continued as the summer wore on. Then, incredible as it may seem, at a time when the Southern Cause in the region seemed doomed beyond recovery, the Confederates scored their largest victory in the Territory since 1861. Cooper was well aware of the massive hay operations that were going on in preparation for feeding the thousands of U.S. cavalry horses and other army livestock during the coming winter. His scouts had also alerted him to the fact that one of the largest U.S. supply wagon trains ever to be sent to Fort Gibson was being assembled at Fort Scott, Kansas. With these things in mind, a strong force of Confederate cavalry was ordered up the valley of the Grand River above Fort Gibson in the middle of September. Eight hundred men of the 1st Indian Cavalry Brigade under Gen. Stand Watie and 1,200 men of newly promoted Gen. Richard Gano's Texas

Brigade were chosen to carry out the mission. Outflanking Union positions on their ride north, the Indians and Texans thundered into the Grand River valley about 15 miles above Fort Gibson with 2,000 troopers and six artillery pieces. There, at Flat Rock Creek, two miles from Grand River, a large Federal hay camp was in operation.

Captain Edgar Barker was in charge of the 125 Union troops engaged in the hay operation at Flat Rock: a detachment of the 2nd Kansas Cavalry and a portion of the 1st Kansas Colored Infantry. Alert to the dangers in the area, Captain Barker kept small cavalry patrols out around the clock, scouting the countryside near his camp. Flat Rock Creek was a small branch of Grand River on the prairie. There were numerous pools connected by narrow threads of water along the clear little stream. The lagoons were lined with small willows and brush: shady, cool retreats for men working hard all day in the sun-baked hay fields. In the afternoon of September 16, one of Captain Barker's scouting patrols came galloping back into camp with horrendous news that hundreds and hundreds of Rebel cavalrymen were heading straight toward Flat Rock. Immediately, Barker ordered his men in from the hay fields. The nervous soldiers grabbed their weapons and accouterments and were deployed to the rear of the camp along a ravine which made a natural defensive trench for a firing line. Then Captain Barker rode out with a small cavalry escort to observe the enemy. Silently he hoped that his scouts had greatly exaggerated what they had seen; perhaps it was only an enemy cavalry detachment briefly passing through the region, on their way someplace else.

Barker rode to the top of a high ridge in the prairie. The horrified Yankee captain didn't need his field glasses to see the 2,000 enemy troops advancing before him. Wheeling their horses about, Barker and his escort rode at breakneck speed back to the Flat Rock camp, closely pursued by their foes. By the time Barker and his escort dismounted and ran to the defensive ravine near their camp, the Texans and Indians had approached within 200 yards and commenced a fierce attack from five different points. During the next half hour, the tiny

Federal force, outnumbered nearly twenty to one, repulsed three Confederate cavalry charges. It was obvious to Barker and his men that they would soon be overrun. The captain then made a difficult command decision: he would mount up all his cavalrymen who could locate their horses, lead them in a desperate charge against the Confederate line, break through the enemy position, and ride to safety. The African-American troops and dismounted cavalrymen would be left behind to fight their way to the Grand River timber if possible. With pistols blazing, Barker and 40 of his men charged directly into a line of Watie's warriors. The captain and 15 of his troopers made it through the enemy line and beat a dusty path to Fort Gibson.

The troops of the 1st Kansas Colored rallied under their lieutenant, Thomas B. Sutherland, for a last stand. Each of them knew their chances of escaping alive were very slim, and they prepared to sell their lives at a very heavy cost to the enemy. Firing their Springfield rifles as rapidly as possible from the poor shelter of their bloody, smoke-filled ravine, they repelled charge after charge as their own numbers grew less and less, just like the ammunition in their cartridge boxes. With their ammunition finally gone, Lieutenant Sutherland gave the order for every man to save himself. They all split up and ran for their lives as the expected massacre commenced. Some who did escape hid underwater in the shallow lagoons with their noses just barely above the surface, concealed by the brush and lily pads. General Gano later wrote of the encounter, "The setting sun witnessed our complete success as its last lingering rays rested upon a field of blood. Seventy three Federals, mostly Negroes, lay dead." The Confederates also burned an estimated three to five thousand tons of hay as well as a government hay-mowing machine before leaving Flat Rock.

The battle-hardened Confederate force moved north on the Texas Road to find the huge Federal supply train which the Southerners knew was en route to Fort Gibson. It consisted of at least 300 wagons with a guard of 260 troopers of the 2nd, 6th, and 14th Kansas Cavalry regiments, and 100 Native American troops of the 3rd Indian Home Guard, all under the command

The cavalry troopers saddled up for a desperate charge,
leaving the black infantrymen to fend for themselves.

of Maj. Henry Hopkins of the 2nd Kansas. While encamped at Horse Creek on September 17, the major received a dispatch from Fort Gibson informing him of a major Confederate advance north and ordering him to take his supply train to Cabin Creek where a Union post had been established with a strong stockade for defense. One hundred seventy Cherokee troops of the 2nd Indian Home Guard manned the post, and 140 additional men of the 3rd Indian Home Guard soon arrived from Fort Gibson as reinforcements. This gave Major Hopkins just over 600 men to defend his wagons as he arrived at the Cabin Creek outpost at noon on September 18. The major then took 25 troopers of his 2nd Kansas with him to scout the region and soon came upon a portion of Gano's Confederate force already occupying a ravine in the prairie south of the post. Hopkins immediately rode back to camp and ordered his wagons parked in close order in the rear of the stockade, strengthened his pickets, and formed his men in line for an attack. According to what he had just seen, and what his scouts reported as well, Major Hopkins believed the enemy force probably did not exceed 800 men and was without artillery.

By midnight General Watie had arrived with the balance of the Confederate troops and artillery. He and General Gano decided to advance on the Union position by the light of the night's full moon. When within about half a mile from the Cabin Creek post, the Confederates deployed for battle. Watie's force was on the left, Gano's force on the right, and the six-gun artillery battery in the center. The long Rebel battle line advanced to within just 300 yards of the Federal position before a blazing volley of Yankee musketry ripped through the night air. The 2,000 Southerners immediately returned fire with their shoulder weapons, revealing the full strength of their force to Major Hopkins who strained his eyes in the moonlight to see their lengthy double lines of numerous troops. Then to the major's utter horror and astonishment, six cannons suddenly roared aloud with a deafening artillery volley from the center of his foe's battle line. Hundreds of iron balls from artillery canister rounds tore through camp tents, timber, and wagons like giant shotgun blasts. Artillery shells exploded in blinding flashes all around the stockade and panicked the supply train's mule teams. Hundreds of the terrified animals broke into a blind stampede and plunged over high bluffs overlooking the creek, taking numerous wagons with them. Most of the teamsters and wagon masters cut mules loose from tangled harnesses and mounted them for a speedy escape north toward Fort Scott. The hellish gunfire continued through the night, and a number of Union soldiers chose to withdraw early from the bloody contest, disappearing into the darkness. Some claimed Major Hopkins himself joined the early retreat, but such allegations were never proven.

At dawn the Confederates gradually maneuvered to partially encircle the Federal force, subjecting the battered Yanks to an effective crossfire. Finally the outnumbered, outgunned Union survivors withdrew from the battlefield, retreating toward Fort Gibson. The victorious Confederates burned the disabled wagons and killed the crippled mules. The remaining 130 wagons and 740 healthy mules were all theirs for the taking. Heavily loaded with clothing, raw foodstuffs, ammunition, and accouterments, the captured supply train transformed the ragged, half-starved Confederate force into a well-fed, properly equipped, and nearly uniformed little army.

The action known as the Second Battle of Cabin Creek, not far from present-day Big Cabin, Oklahoma, convinced people on both sides that the Confederates in Indian Territory were not a weak, defeated rabble of washed-up warriors, but rather a dangerous force of hardened veterans who were still a threat to the Federal government. Despite the horrendous cannonading and heavy musketry during the battle, casualties were light due to the fact that most men on both sides spent the major portion of the action lying down in a prone position behind logs, in ravines, and—in the case of the Union force—under the protective cover of the slanting bluff below the camp. The Federals had only 7 men killed, 6 wounded, and 24 missing. It is not known how many citizen teamsters were casualties. Gano's brigade of Texans suffered 8 dead and 37 wounded. Watie did not give a full report of his losses, listing only the number of

*Terrified mule teams panicked
and broke into a blind stampede.*

his officers who were casualties: one killed and four wounded.

After fitting up as many mule teams as possible to remove the captured wagonloads of supplies, the victorious Confederate raiders started south. That evening at Pryor Creek, Gano and Watie ran headlong into a strong force of Union infantry which was making a forced march from Fort Gibson to reinforce Major Hopkins at Cabin Creek. The Union commander was none other than Col. James M. Williams who had led the 1st Kansas Colored Infantry to victory at the First Battle of Cabin Creek. Now Williams faced the victors of the Second Battle of Cabin Creek. His force consisted of elements of the 1st and 2nd Kansas Colored Infantry as well as the 11th U.S. Colored Infantry Regiment with a battery of highly accurate, long-range, rifled artillery pieces known as Parrott Rifles. Colonel Williams, outnumbered about two to one, fell back to a better defensive position and, as soon as the advancing Southerners came within range, opened fire with his Parrott guns. The powerful, deadly artillery pieces drove back the Confederate advance. Gano and Watie unlimbered their artillery, and the batteries of both sides dueled for an hour until dusk when Gano deployed most of his troops in a long battle line on a high ridge in the prairie. While this impressive display of force was being staged in full view of Williams and his men, the captured supply wagons from Cabin Creek were being rushed forward behind the lines, heading southwest toward the Verdigris River. That night the Confederates built fires along the ridge to create the appearance that they were encamped in force. At dawn Colonel Williams saw that his foes were long gone. Williams' troops had marched 80 miles in less than two days and were in no condition to pursue their foes, especially when they were outnumbered anyway. Gano and Watie crossed the Verdigris near Claremore Mound, then rode to the Arkansas River which they crossed at Tulsey Town.

The weary Confederates arrived at Camp Bragg on the south side of the Canadian River on September 28. They had ridden over 400 miles in 14 days and whipped the U.S. Army in a fierce little battle that would prove to be the Federal government's worst defeat in Indian Territory. Their military action also turned out to be the last serious clash between the armed forces of the Union and the Confederacy in the Territory.

Although Southern sympathizers were greatly encouraged by the stunning victory of Watie and Gano at Cabin Creek, the Federals soon replaced their losses and resupplied Fort Gibson, with no further grand assaults by their foes. It was at last becoming obvious in the region, as it was in the rest of the country as well, that the Federals had unlimited resources and manpower. It was simply inevitable that they would eventually win the war.

Many dreaded the coming of spring, bringing a new season of deadly military campaigns and terrifying guerrilla raids. Yet the spring of 1865 was not the same as the previous four. Instead of countless volleys of gunfire, there were only a few scattered shots, and most of those didn't hit any targets. Not even the legendary Stand Watie took to the field in one of his daring raids. Both sides, sick of death and destruction, preferred to keep their distance from each other, awaiting the unavoidable events which would soon put an end to all the madness. News would eventually arrive in the Territory of Gen. Robert E. Lee's surrender at Appomattox, Virginia, on April 9. Interestingly, a Native American officer was present at the historic proceedings back East. Colonel Ely S. Parker, a full-blood member of the Seneca Tribe, served on the staff of none other than Gen. Ulysses S. Grant. As a matter of fact, Colonel Parker was one of only a few Union officers present in the parlor of the McLean home where Lee signed the surrender papers. As Grant's military secretary, it was Parker who drafted the official copy of the terms of surrender for the generals' signatures.

After Lee surrendered the Army of Northern Virginia at Appomattox, armed resistance to Federal authority rapidly crumbled as other generals throughout the South surrendered their armies as well. One last skirmish took place in Indian Territory as three Confederate cavalrymen were blown out of their saddles in a hail of gunfire along Snake Creek in the Choctaw Nation on April 24, 1865. The clash took place when a Federal cavalry patrol out of Fort Gibson ran headlong into a small detachment of Southern troopers carrying military mail north from Boggy Depot. An inspection of the captured letters revealed that these Confederates and their comrades had not yet heard of Lee's surrender. Finally, on May 26, the military forces of the Confederate Trans-Mississippi Department were formally surrendered "on paper" in New Orleans by Gen. E. Kirby Smith's chief of staff, Gen. Simon Buckner. General Douglas Cooper followed suit and surrendered all white Confederate soldiers in Indian Territory. His Native American troops reserved the right to surrender separately from white soldiers, since their tribes had entered the war as independent allies of the Confederacy. As a matter of fact, in a letter to General Buckner, General Cooper stated that it was not only impractical for him to surrender the Indian forces, but that his life would be endangered if he attempted to do so.

Finally, on June 19 at Doaksville, capital of the Choctaw Nation, the Confederate military forces of that tribe were surrendered by their new principal chief, Peter Pitchlynn. Four days later, on June 23, near the same place, Gen. Stand Watie at last surrendered his hard-riding Cherokee troopers, together with the Creek and Seminole forces, as well as the Osage Battalion. The Cherokee general surrendered to Lt. Col. A. C. Matthews who had been sent south with a detachment of U.S. cavalry to seek him out. Watie was the last Confederate general in the American Civil War to surrender his command. Confederate Chickasaw and Caddo warriors made their surrender official on July 14, over three months after Appomattox. At last, the Civil War in Indian Territory had come to an end.

Today as one stands in present-day Oklahoma and surveys the beauty of the landscape and experiences the hospitality of its people, it is hard to imagine the cruel war which raged across the region so long ago. Yet there is a practical value in recalling those rough old days: remembering such a violent era in our history helps us to better appreciate the quality of our lives today. We can also draw a good deal of inspiration to overcome our own problems in day-to-day life when we consider the tremendous courage and fortitude required of those who endured the fire and fury of the Civil War in Indian Territory.

Bibliography

Bearss, Edwin C. "The Civil War Comes to Indian Territory, 1861: The Flight of Opothleyoholo." *Journal of the West*. Vol. XI, No. 1, January 1972. Los Angeles, CA: Lorrin L. Morrison and Carroll Spear Morrison, 1972.

Britton, Wiley. *The Civil War on the Border 1861-1862*. Vol. I. New York: G. P. Putnam's Sons, the Knickerbocker Press, 1899.

Britton, Wiley. *The Civil War on the Border 1863-1865*. Vol. II. New York: G. P. Putnam's Sons, the Knickerbocker Press, 1899.

Carle, Glenn L. "The First Kansas Colored." *Civil War Chronicles*. Vol. 3, No. 3, Winter 1994. New York: American Heritage, 1994.

Connelley, William Elsey. *Quantrill and the Border Wars*. Cedar Rapids, IA: The Torch Press, 1910.

Connelley, William Elsey. *The Life of Preston B. Plumb*. Chicago: Browne & Howell Company, 1913.

Cornish, Dudley Taylor. *The Sable Arm*. Lawrence, KS: University Press of Kansas, 1987.

Cunningham, Frank. *General Stand Watie's Confederate Indians*. San Antonio, TX: The Naylor Company, 1959.

Fischer, Leroy H. and Gill, Jerry. *Confederate Indian Forces Outside of Indian Territory*. Norman, OK: University of Oklahoma Press, 1969.

Fischer, Leroy H. *The Battle of Honey Springs*. Norman, OK: University of Oklahoma Printing Services, 1988.

Franks, Kenny A. *Stand Watie and the Agony of the Cherokee Nation*. Memphis, TN: Memphis State University Press, 1979.

Gaines, W. Craig. *The Confederate Cherokees: John Drew's Regiment of Mounted Rifles.* Baton Rouge, LA: Louisiana State University Press, 1989.

Hatcher, Richard W., III and Piston, William Garrett, editors. *Kansans at Wilson's Creek.* Springfield, MO: Wilson's Creek National Battlefield Foundation, 1993.

Huff, James Paul. "Fort Scott's Regiment: The Sixth Kansas Volunteer Cavalry 1861-1865." Unpublished thesis, Pittsburg State University, Pittsburg, KS: 1987.

Ingenthron, Elmo. *Borderland Rebellion.* Branson, MO: The Ozarks Mountaineer, 1980.

Josephy, Alvin M. *The Civil War in the American West.* New York: Alfred A. Knopf, 1991.

Knight, Wilfred. *Red Fox.* Glendale, CA: The Arthur H. Clark Company, 1988.

Monaghan, Jay. *Civil War on the Western Border: 1865-1865.* New York: Little, Brown and Company, 1955.

Payne, Curtis, "Battle of Boggy Depot, the Indian Nations." *The Western Campaigner.* January 1994. Waukomis, OK: The Missouri Civil War Reenactors Association, 1994.

Rampp, Lary C. "Confederate Indian Sinking of the 'J.R. Williams.'" *Journal of the West.* Vol. XI, No. 1, January 1972. Los Angeles, CA: Lorrin L. Morrison and Carroll Spear Morrison, 1972.

Rosewitz, Paul R. "Action at Ft. Gibson: May 20, 1863." *The Western Campaigner.* October 1983. Kansas City, MO: The Missouri Civil War Reenactors Association, 1983.

Schrantz, Ward L. *Jasper County, Missouri in the Civil War.* Carthage, MO: The Carthage Press, 1923.

Shoemaker, Arthur. "Hard Rope's Civil War." *Civil War Times Illustrated.* September/October 1990. Harrisonburg, PA: Historical Times, Inc., 1990.

Steele, Phillip W. and Cottrell, Steve. *Civil War in the Ozarks.* Gretna, LA: Pelican Publishing Company, 1993.

Thoburn, Joseph B. *A Standard History of Oklahoma.* Vol. I. Chicago: The American Historical Society, 1916.

Woodward, Grace Steele. *The Cherokees.* Norman, OK: University of Oklahoma Press, 1963.

Index to Battles
and Skirmishes